'Ted Buxton is a football ma̱[...] ̱He has lived and breathed the game we all k[...] ̱. He is also one of the kindest and most loyal men [...] ̱and I am honoured to call him my friend'

Terry Venables

'Ted is an old-school football legend and has lived an eventful life. I know that this book will give anyone interested in football or sport more generally, a fascinating insight into life behind the scenes in this great game'

Frank Lampard OBE

'Ted Buxton is a real football man, a great character with experience of the game second to none. He has worked at all levels from the base of the pyramid to the top and his stories are a must read for any football lover'

Gordon Taylor OBE, Chief Executive, PFA

'Ted Buxton was my chief scout at Millwall FC and the Tampa Bay Rowdies in the NASL USA. His ability to select and recommend players at both clubs assisted us in gaining promotion with Millwall FC from the English Third Division to the Second Division and Reaching two finals of the NASL and winning the NASL Indoor Championship. His added ability of scouting and first class reports on opponents was also so valuable in our success over many years'

Gordon Jago MBE

'Ted Buxton is someone I have known for a very long time and he's football from grass roots upwards. He has always had many a tale to tell, and his book is the ultimate behind-the-scenes for every football fan'

Roy Hodgson

'Ted Buxton is a really, really good man. He is what every football club wants and needs. With Ted there is never a dull moment, and his glass is always half full'

Steve Bruce

'Ted was a great help to me throughout our time at Tampa Bay Rowdies and then subsequently at Gillingham. He has always been positive and definite in his opinion of the players – a great quality for a chief scout to have. He is an excellent judge of a good player, and has been a loyal and trustworthy friend for thirty-seven years. He was such a big asset to have around the players and in the dressing room area, as he always had a great story to tell – he was a real character'

Keith Peacock

TED BUXTON

MY LIFE IN FOOTBALL

Best wishes

Ted Buxton

RedDoor

Published by RedDoor
www.reddoorpublishing.com

ISBN 978-1-910453-41-4

A CIP catalogue record for this book is available
from the British Library

Cover design: Clare Connie Shepherd www.paintedbyclare.com
Typesetting: Tutis Innovative E-Solutions Pte. Ltd
Printed in Great Britain by Bell and Bain Ltd., Glasgow, UK

Dedicated to my sister, Edie, and brother-in-law, John, who have always been there for me

CONTENTS

MY FRIEND, TED BUXTON

When I was a young player of seventeen, having just broken into Chelsea's first team, I still couldn't get enough of football. Whenever I wasn't playing, I would always attend other matches all over London. It became a bit of a joke between Bernard Joy, a senior football journalist for the London Evening Standard, and me, as he would always find me at games. Bernard happened to be a great player himself and even represented England as an amateur player.

Bernard recognised well enough what I was doing at such games, as I felt you could only really learn about football by watching as much of it as possible. Consequently, I was always watching matches even when I didn't have to, and I always learned something from every game I saw.

Ted Buxton knows this only too well and I suspect there aren't many people alive who have seen as much live football as him. Even now his appetite for watching games at every level is still there for everyone to see, and I reckon he has probably seen more matches than almost anyone I know.

He is one of the straightest, and most honest men you could ever meet and as soon as I met him, it felt as if I had known him all my life.

I always found his judgement on players to be absolutely spot on. His advice and insights came with no frills attached, as he had this great ability to keep it simple and to the point.

TED BUXTON - MY LIFE IN FOOTBALL

I had absolutely no hesitation in making him my chief scout at Tottenham and also at England, and as a man, the players loved him. With his barrel chest and deep-throated laughter, and sheer passion for the game of football we love, it is little wonder he attracted such admiration from players everywhere.

It wasn't, however, just for his humour that players responded to him – it was also for his sheer knowledge of the game. There was many a time when a shrewd word in a player's ear by Ted at half-time has transformed a second half performance.

His tactical understanding of football was also exceptional. Any of you who might have had the pleasure of reading one of his scouting reports will know exactly what I mean. They were concise, insightful and always revealed both the strengths and weaknesses of a team.

One of the proudest moments of both of our lives came during Euro '96 after England's 4–1 destruction of Holland. Sir Stanley Matthews came up to Ted as they were leaving Wembley and said 'Ted, tell Terry that that was one of the greatest England performances I've ever seen at Wembley, and I would have loved to have played in that team'.

Ted Buxton is a football man through and through. He has lived and breathed the game we all love at every level. He can get as much enjoyment from spotting talented youngsters, as working at international level with some of the greatest professionals.

He is also one of the kindest and most loyal men I know, and I am honoured to call him my friend.

Terry Venables, September 2017

FOREWORD

When Ted first asked if I would write a contribution to his book, I had no hesitation whatsoever in putting pen to paper. After all, how could I refuse the man who showed such faith in me from the very beginning?

Since I was a young kid, Ted has been an integral part of my football career. In the early days at the West Ham Academy, Ted came to watch me play – a lot. In fact he watched so many games I'm amazed he didn't get sick of the sight of me! His commitment was and still is, second to none.

So from an early age I was lucky to have someone as knowledgeable and dependable as Ted. He offered me invaluable advice and support, both on and off the pitch. Rising up through the ranks at the Academy, I took quite a lot of stick from the West Ham crowd because of my family ties. Ted was on hand to constantly reassure me, telling me not to worry – he really helped me to handle the situation, which was a pretty tough one for a teenager.

During Euro '96, whilst Ted worked alongside Terry Venables in charge of the England team, he played a major part in inviting me to train with the full squad at their training camp just outside London. I found the experience incredible and a huge factor in my development. Ted's part in arranging this, and his words of wisdom throughout the week I spent with the team, will always be in my mind and are hugely appreciated as I look back.

Ted always knew I could work harder and achieve more. Thinking about it, I probably was playing too defensively at the time, and I remember that Ted mentioned this to my dad, Frank Senior, and that he thought I could break in beyond the main striker. And I did – and that's when I started being an attacking number 8, breaking beyond the main forwards and soon began to score goals. It was a good set up and obviously Ted had the foresight to predict it.

This is my personal experience of working with Ted, but I know he has helped, guided and supported many like me. The fact that he is still so involved with his local football team, particularly the youth side at Chalfont, shows that his commitment to the game goes far beyond just a job. He is an old-school football legend and has lived an eventful life. I know that this book will give anyone interested in football or sport more generally, a fascinating insight into life behind the scenes in this great game.

Frank Lampard OBE, September 2017

DEATH IN THE JUNGLE

It was a typical hot and steamy afternoon in the jungle of Malaya. The terrain was rugged and the sweat was pouring from the lads, including me, all no more than boys, who had been asked to be men in our National Service tour of duty in 1952. But in Malaya, you had to grow up fast. You had to do things, hear things and see things that you never would have thought would have been part of your life.

We six rookies had set out at first light. We headed for the highest ridge around the target area and there we were to watch and listen. By the time it had got to midday, we had gone far enough. Leeches were everywhere all over our bodies and could only be prised off using a burning cigarette. But after six months in the jungle, we were used to that kind of nuisance. We settled down about 200 yards from the rubber plantation where it was anticipated that the Communist terrorists (CTs) would arrive. At the top of the ridge, we could just see the tops of the rubber trees. I had acclimatised quicker than most to the demands of this terrain and climate – perhaps it was something to do with surviving my tough South East London childhood in the years before and during the Second World War. You had to be strong to come through that. You had to learn quickly to just stay alive – and I took that lesson with me to Malaya.

'Let's eat,' I said. You had to choose the right time and place to eat out there because the smell from the food would carry for miles through the jungle. But at our high vantage point, I knew we would be safe. 'The smell will rise up,' I said to other members of the patrol (Bob, Jackie, Sammy, our wireless operator, and our medic, who was a baker in civvy street so nicknamed George the Baker). We had tinned stew and rice and it went down well. Curry powder was a great asset – it smothered any of the rancid taste of the rations. Sammy and I had the first watch. Then it was the turn of Bob and Jack. I put my head down and no sooner had I got settled when a twig hit me on the stomach. I assumed it was broken by one of the monkeys who were indulging in their normal antics in the trees above us.

Then I looked up and saw Bob pointing down. I gently touched Sammy to wake him and we crawled over to Bob and Jack. Climbing the hills were two CTs. We had a clear view of them and we could hear them as they made their way up the hill. The sweat was pouring off them and they were gasping for breath. That is what the Malayan jungle does to you when you exert yourself.

We lined them up in our sights. I gestured that I would open up the firing. The two CTs were only about five yards apart and the others opened up after me. They didn't know what hit them. When the firing had stopped, we waited to see if there would be any reaction from either of them. The silence was eerie. Then there was a cry of pain and we moved towards them slowly. One CT was dead; the other badly hit in the stomach with his guts hanging out and he was in agony. The medic took some morphine from his pack to give him a shot to help dull his obvious pain. We put a field dressing around his stomach and the morphine began to kick in – but he was still in a bad way. We hurriedly covered over the body of the dead CT and decided to try to take the other back to base camp. A poncho was tied around him, we tied a pole to it and we got ready to carry him. Sammy and I were to be the first to carry him with Bob leading and Jack bringing up the rear. But in that heat, through the unforgiving jungle, it would be hard work.

The light was starting to fade and then the CT started to moan more and more because of the pain.

We gave him the last of the morphine. Now we had a problem. Treating the wounded man had slowed us up no end. 'We are never going to get back before dark,' said Bob and it was hard to argue with him. We would have to camp overnight but the CT's cries of pain would alert other bandits in the area to our exact position. They would be sure to be waiting for us at first light so it was putting us all in danger.

'Someone is going to have to put him away,' I said. 'Any volunteers?'

The silence was deafening. Killing someone in a fire fight is one thing. You know it is ultimately him or you. This was a whole new world for me and the others. I looked at the CT. He was in a bad way and it was clear that he wouldn't survive but would take time to die in agony. His breathing was shallow and his moaning was becoming more intense. There was no more morphine, precious little water and the medic could do nothing for him.

The CT looked up at me with eyes that reflected the depth of his pain. He had just about enough strength to signal that he wanted a drink. Sammy put a couple of packs behind him to prop him up and stop him falling back. He held a tin cup of water to moisten his lips but the CT just coughed it back. I walked behind him. The others turned away.

I shot him from behind the left ear and the bullet went straight through his brain. He slumped forward. I just stared, almost in disbelief. I felt numb. I was shaking and sweating at the same time. Everything was still with not a sound from insects, monkeys or anything. It seemed like an eternity before anyone said a word.

'It had to be done,' someone said and to this day I cannot remember who it was but it was no comfort to me. Suddenly I, a young man who was still in his teens, had become a self-appointed hit man. I kept telling myself it was a necessity, that my actions had cost one life but had probably saved six others – including my own. I kept trying to convince myself of that but it was to be many, many years before the recurring nightmares about that moment would stop. He may have been a terrorist who would not have thought twice about killing me, but I couldn't help thinking that he was someone's son and probably a father as well, with a wife and kids at home. Somehow, I shook off the effects of the moment. There was still work to be done. I snapped myself out of the nightmare by concentrating on the present. 'OK, let's take his mug shot and get him buried,' I said, very sharply.

We stayed awake most of the night and in the morning we took the two CTs' weapons and some papers written in Chinese that might yield valuable information back at base. The humidity was horrendous as we climbed upwards so that we could move high along the ridges, where the jungle was less dense and where we would be at an advantage in case of attack. The top of the ridges was deep with elephant dung, heavy with the flies attracted by the stench, but we eventually made it back to base.

In the debrief with Captain Langhorn, I told him that one CT had been killed outright and the other died while we were preparing to get him back. The others backed up my story. Then came the shock. We were ordered to go back and get the bodies we had buried because HQ needed the bodies for some kind of verification of their identity.

We were all sent back by truck to the area with a Sarawak tracker and a couple of other lads from the platoon. With the help of the tracker and our map reference we located the bodies and carried them back to the truck.

As soon as we got back and he saw the second body, Langhorn was suspicious.

'Corporal,' he said in a stern and officious tone. This meant he was serious. 'How come you bothered trying to get that bastard back to camp with half his gut blown away plus his brains blown out? What really happened, Buck?' I explained everything.

'OK,' he said. 'We'll play it your way. I'll report the Commies were killed outright and buried together.' I thanked him. 'You have done a good job, you and the rest. Well done,' he said.

I felt better but I was to be haunted by what had happened that night in the jungle for many years to come. I could not get the man's face out of my mind. But it was war – kill or be killed. Normal life was on hold.

AN EAST END BOY

What I want to do in this book is to tell the story of my life, a fantastic one because I have been involved in the sport that I love the most – football. And it has been an astonishing journey: starting out as a South London butcher, I ended up working with the England team and some of the most famous names in the world. From my days as a kid in south-east London, I have been fascinated by the game and I have been able to travel all over the world and work with many of the top names in the sport – Bobby Robson, Paul Gascoigne, Gary Lineker, Terry Venables and Gordon Jago to name just a few – and also, of course, with great pride, with the England team. I have been from Madrid to Manchuria, from Florida to the Far East. It has been a pleasure and a privilege every step of the way. And along the way I also became acquainted with an array of characters including the notorious Kray twins, Reggie and Ronnie.

But for me to grow up to become the man, I had to go through a very tough childhood in which violence was a part of everyday life. The survival instinct was bred in me from early on, which is why I was able to despatch that unfortunate CT, even though it turned my stomach to do so. You could not escape when you were brought up in London during the war. All you heard, all day every day, were guns and bombs.

We grew up in Achilles Street in New Cross – a typical tight-knit community in the 'wrong' part of London – with my mum and dad, my brother Alf and sister Edie. I was the youngest. My dad's brother and his wife lived in the same street; neighbours were all called uncles and aunts. Everyone knew everyone else and you could leave your doors open or with a key attached to a piece of string inside the letter box. Everyone was poor so there was nothing to steal and the only thieving would be when someone tried to break into the local pub to get beer or into the tanning factory above the stables where the brewery kept its dray horses, which were used to deliver barrels of beer.

The neighbourhood coppers were always on their beat handling any disturbances in the area and were part of the local community. As kids, we were always brought up to respect them and they were good at keeping everything under control so, although it was a rough area, it was still a safe place to live. During the summertime everyone would sit outside their front doors and the kids had a lot of freedom. We were encouraged to play football and cricket in the roads where there was hardly any traffic as no one had a car.

I was five years old when the Second World War broke out. The first vivid memories I have of that time were being sat down by my mum and dad at home to be told that we were to be evacuated to the country to a place called Barcombe in Sussex, a place that sounded a million miles away to a very young child. I didn't want to go but was reassured by my brother and sister that the three of us would stay together.

By the morning of the departure, plans had already changed because Alfie, being older at fourteen, told us that he didn't have to go and was staying behind to help the fire brigade. Edie and I were told to assemble at the Childeric Primary School in New Cross with the other evacuees. We were all deloused with lousing powder administered by the school nurse and then badged up with labels just like those put on parcels for delivery. To a tearful farewell from mum, dad having already gone to work, we were marched up in lines to New Cross station. Dad hadn't been able to stay to say goodbye as he had to go off early to work on the trams. All the kids were lined up outside the station ready to be boarded on the trains, when a No. 72 tram stopped abruptly outside the station. All the kids looked over and then I saw my dad, who was a conductor on the tram, jumping off. He ran over to give my sister and me a big farewell cuddle. He hadn't let us go without saying goodbye, after all. Then we were off.

As the train passed through different towns on the line, various groups of children got off – until we got to Lewes in Sussex. There, we were told to disembark and get on a coach with a group of other children who were also to be sent off to their allocated families. At one of the villages, Edie and I were told to get off and found ourselves with a farming family: a farmer, his wife and a daughter in her twenties. They were not particularly welcoming and clearly didn't want us to be there but were happy with the money being paid to them by the government for the privilege of housing us, the evacuees.

We were put into the local school. We were not welcome there either. I didn't understand why I had to be there so I was miserable and probably not on my best behaviour. There were several other evacuees in the school so we formed a kind of clique and didn't fit in very well with the local children. They seemed to look down on us and we in turn found them snooty so we were frequently in trouble and, even at that early age, I ended up being caned quite a few times. Caning didn't work because it just made me more resentful.

Back on the farm, things were no better. The daughter was always slipping off to meet a local lad when she was supposed to be keeping an eye on us. We were not fed too well and were always sent to bed early and hungry and were forced to attend the local church on Sunday, which we had never done at home.

After Edie and I endured this for about a month, it seemed things might improve when Alfie arrived to join us but this did not last long. Ironically, given that he had been working with them in London, the fire brigade had to be called out to the farm after Alfie had been smoking in his bed and set light to the mattress. His safety-first training clearly hadn't sunk in. After this, Alfie was packed off back to London and Edie and I were again left on our own, even more unwelcome than we had been before.

Events came to a head when Edie and I were sent alone to church on a Sunday morning. I was starving hungry and blackberries were ripe in the bushes on the way back from church. I crammed berries hungrily into my mouth and wiped my hands on my white shirt. When we got back to the farm, the farmer's wife went mad and slapped me violently around the head when she saw my shirt. Edie jumped to my defence and we were both sent to our room and told that, as a punishment, we wouldn't get anything at all to eat.

That was the last straw. Edie started planning our escape. The next morning, she packed all of our clothes in her school bag and, instead of going to school, we slipped out past the farmer's wife and raced for the bus stop where we boarded the first bus to take us to Barcombe station. Edie had enough money for the bus but we didn't have any money for a train to take us home. So we waited until no one was watching and jumped onto the train to Lewes. We changed trains at Lewes again without anyone spotting us and we got all the way to New Cross before a ticket inspector stopped us and asked for our tickets.

Of course we had no tickets and he could see that we had no means of paying for our fares. Edie pleaded with him and told him that our dad would pay. She hastily wrote down our name and address and begged the inspector not to send us back. He seemed very stern but, not knowing what to do with us, delivered us to the guard at New Cross. Fortunately, Edie's pleading found a soft spot in the guard, who then let us go on the promise that my dad would pay the fare later. Knowing how honest my dad was, I have always assumed that he went back later to pay the fare.

It was now early afternoon as Edie and I walked down the street towards home. Some of the neighbours called out to us and asked what we were doing home. Edie told them proudly that we had escaped. When we walked in through the front door, mum was busy, with her back to us, scrubbing the lino on the kitchen floor. She was surprised to hear someone coming into the house and got a shock when she turned round and looked up to see the two children that she thought were safely down in Sussex. But there were hugs all round.

Mum was all for sending us back to Sussex for safety because the Battle of Britain was raging but, on hearing Edie's tales of our experiences as evacuees, dad decided that we were better off taking our chances with the daily risks with German bombs and staying with the family in London.

Living within a stone's throw from Surrey Docks, all you could hear, all day, every day, were guns, bombs and sirens, followed by the all-clear, when people would emerge from the shelters to find out what had happened to their street.

I don't know why but I never felt any fear. It seemed normal to stroll through the streets in the morning picking up pieces of shrapnel and then swapping them at school with the other boys for bigger, better pieces. We didn't even get excited hearing that streets had been bombed and simply accepted the fact that kids had not turned up for school when their streets had been hit.

The danger was brought home to me by one memorable incident when my father was walking me home with my schoolmate, Tommy Davey. As we rounded the wall at the corner of our street, the sirens sounded to warn of an air raid and I stared wide-eyed to see a German plane coming out of the sky towards us, blazing away with its guns. My dad grabbed the two of us, pulled us back into the doorway of the doctor's surgery and fell on top of us as bullets strafed the walls. As I peered out I could see the pilot with his head gear and goggles as he sped off, quickly followed by one of our fighter planes. As quickly as it happened, it was all over. We heard later that he had dropped bombs around the dock area and made a quick getaway, but not before he had killed six children around Catford School. When I went back years later, the bullet holes were still visible in that wall as a chilling reminder of how close I came as a child to having my story end there.

During one heavy air-raid, the sirens had sounded early and everyone had packed into the community shelter under the stables. It was stifling in there amid the smell of bodies and the stables above so, when there was a brief lull in the firing of the ack-ack guns before the next wave of bombers came over, I was more than happy to be sent out to the pub next door to collect a jug of water. I climbed the steps out of the shelter, carrying a tin jug, and scurried across the cobble stones in darkness to go into the back door of the pub, which was always kept unlocked. I thought everyone was down in the shelter so, when I opened the pub door, I was surprised to see that an oil lamp was already lit.

I wasn't the only one taken by surprise because as I entered the room, there was Bill, the local air raid protection (ARP) warden, having it off across the bar with the pub landlady. Her skirt was up and I could see her white drawers so I knew something was going on. Kids in those days, however, didn't get the sex education that kids get today so it was still a bit of mystery to me. Seeing a wide-eyed seven year old at the door must have put Bill off his stroke but he quickly recovered, straightened up and explained, 'She's got a bad back, young Eddie.' I accepted that, collected my water and hurried back to the shelter, as the ack-ack started and I heard the planes droning overhead.

I thought no more about the incident until sometime later when I overheard some of the adults gossiping about Bill and the landlady and put two and two together, but I didn't tell anyone else what I had stumbled upon. Years later after the war, when the landlady's husband had returned home and I came home on leave from my national service, Bill was always very generous and used to pop a half crown into my hand and tell me to treat myself. My reward, no doubt, for continuing to keep quiet.

With the Blitz in full force, my parents decided to send me and Edie along with one of her friends to stay for a month with my grandfather, his second wife and their sons, Adam and Peter, on their farm in Berwick-on-Tweed.

It was the first time I had met my grandfather, Peter Brown, but I had heard a lot about him because he had been decorated in the First World War. He had been a sergeant major in the Dardanelles in charge of a burial party that was burying their dead when the Turks had opened fire. He grabbed his shovel as it was his only weapon to hand, charged one of the Turks and killed him with the implement.

After the war and his return to Berwick, he had retained his reputation as a strong man, as hard as nails. He was a heavily built bloke and when he had been into Berwick for a drink during the day, everyone in the village knew to keep out of his way because he could be cantankerous and very intimidating.

I admired him as, despite his fearsome reputation, he was a fair man and he seemed to dote on me and I always felt protected when I was with him. He had served with the King's Own Scottish Borderers along with Piper Daniel Laidlaw, who had earned the Victoria Cross in the Battle of Loos during the First World War, and who coincidentally lived in the same village. They used to meet up and swap tales of their wartime exploits, and I listened. So perhaps it was the influence of my grandfather and those hours of sitting fascinated by the tales of his wartime exploits that made it easy for me to adjust to army life later when I had to do my own national service.

Country life was hard in those days. There was no running water, so we had to fetch the stuff from the village tap which was shared by everyone. We would fill two buckets of water on a harness and carry it back, just as we see pictures of African villagers doing nowadays. The toilet was a wooden seat above a dry hole in the ground that had to be cleaned out from time to time.

The family kept a pig and as a small boy I used to enjoy feeding it until one day I was shocked when they slaughtered it in front of me. The local shepherd came with a massive hammer that he used to knock the pig out and then its throat was cut. I was upset but my grandfather put his arm around me and told me that I had to get used to it because they needed to eat and that was their way of life.

I saw a kinder side in my grandfather's treatment of animals some days later when my uncle Adam was driving a cart filled with hay into the farm and he started slapping the horse, a black and white dray horse called Duke, to make it go up the hill. As Adam passed by the window of their stone farmhouse, my grandfather suddenly shot out of his chair and rushed outside into the yard, where he dragged Adam from the cart and slung him against the wall, swearing at him to leave the horse alone. I watched from the doorway as he made Adam get back on the cart and then my grandfather led the horse by its bridle as he gently coaxed it to plod up the hill.

While I was staying in Berwick I was sent to the local school for a few weeks and it was there that I had my first encounter with organised games of football. Adam then took me to see my very first football match and I can still remember that it was Berwick playing against Tweedmouth. I didn't know it at the time but that was to be the start of a lifetime's involvement with the game.

EARLY DAYS

When I returned to Deptford, the Battle of Britain was over but London was now suffering under the onslaught of the 'flying bombs', the V1s. Around Surrey Docks, we would hear them coming overhead as they made a whining sound. Then the engine would go silent and we knew that it would be about to explode so we would all dive for cover. The V2s were worse because we had no warning that they were were on their way.

As well as using the communal shelters under the stables, my father had erected an Anderson shelter in our own garden so sometimes we would go there. The shelter was half dug into the ground with earth piled on top where my father grew flowers and vegetables. It was dank and musty inside and during the bombing we would sit in there in the glow of an oil lamp with my dad listening to his battery radio.

Schooling during the war years was spasmodic, constantly disrupted by air raids, but the teachers did the best they could and gave the pupils homework projects that we could do while we sat in the shelters. Consequently, I had only a basic education but it was good enough to see me through.

In the lulls between the air raids, the sports teacher would organise football competitions with six-a-side teams, but we didn't have any proper equipment. The ball wouldn't even be a normal football and some of the time we were reduced to playing with a tennis ball, which actually helped to develop ball skills. The teacher even established a mini-league, awarding two points for a win and a point for a draw, encouraging competitiveness, but the games were frequently interrupted by air raid warnings when we all had to dash into the school cellars.

As the war progressed, the bombings became fewer and we could spend more time outdoors playing football. I had trials for the district, at that time Greenwich and Deptford district, which is now Blackheath, and was selected to play. I was an aggressive centre forward and the game was tougher than it is nowadays. The pitches were muddy and the ball was a laced-leather ball that, when wet, weighed pounds.

Scouts from Dulwich Hamlet always watched the district games and as a result I was invited to join what would now be called Dulwich Hamlet's academy. That was the point, at fourteen, when I first felt I had a chance to become a professional footballer.

My father was a Charlton supporter but he was proud that I was picked to play for the district and even more so when I was picked for Dulwich Hamlet. He would go into the pub telling all his friends about his footballer son, while I, being too young to go into a pub, had to sit outside with a lemonade and a biscuit. Sadly, around that time my father's health began to suffer. He was taken into hospital and we were told that they couldn't find anything wrong with him, but he died not too long afterwards. I am glad that at least he lived long enough to see me start my career in football, though he didn't live long enough to see me join the army, which I believe would have made him immensely proud, because he had fought in the infantry in the First World War in the Queen's Royal Regiment.

A year later, my sister, Edie, announced that she was going to marry John, who my father had said was an unsuitable match as he was a spiv from Peckham, which was a notorious area at the time. He'd said John would be no good for her and the marriage wouldn't last, but they have not been apart from that day forth. They are still together sixty-nine years later and John is still my best mate. Unfortunately, I am not in any of the wedding photographs because I never actually made it to the ceremony. I was to play in a game at Dulwich Hamlet on their wedding day and should have got back in time for the photos but football had to come first. I still joke that I wasn't missed at the ceremony – and my sister responds that football was more important to me than her wedding.

John, my new brother-in-law, worked in Leadenhall Market as a greengrocer and my brother, Alf, worked there as a fishmonger. John got me a job in Morris's the Butchers in the market, my first job. I had to push a big barrow with two big wheels and one small one at the front. My role was to collect the orders and push them all round the city, delivering to companies for their kitchens. It took me about a week to find my way around as I kept getting lost, and had to keep asking people directions to find my way back to Leadenhall Market.

At a youth team game at Dulwich against one of the college teams, I had a good game and scored a couple of goals. As I came off the pitch with Wally Wilson, a mate of mine who was quite a good defender, a stranger called me over. He introduced himself to me as a scout from Millwall and offered me a trial at Millwall. I was surprised but understandably excited. When I returned to the dressing room and told Wally, he wanted to come along with me. My life would have turned out totally differently if Wally had been offered the trial that day instead of me.

After the trial I started with Millwall as a ground staff boy. Compared with today's apprentices, being a ground staff boy was really a form of slave labour. We had to help the groundsmen, clean the professionals' boots, paint the terraces, clean the dressing rooms and in between got a bit of coaching and training in small-sided games.

At the age of seventeen I signed a one-year contract to play with Millwall. In those days we didn't see a ball for the first three weeks as all the training was running to get us physically fit and test our stamina. We would have to run up and down the steps of the stands in the ground. Then we would run from the Old Den at Millwall, through Deptford then up Blackheath Hill, a one-in-seven hill. The trainer would be on his bike beside us until he reached the hill when he would get off to push it up. We would be struggling to run up the hill as the tram going up would come alongside us. Inside the tram would be the first team players, including Jack and George Fisher, Frank Neary and Len Tyler. They would wave as they went past, then get off the tram at the top and start their run downhill across Blackheath back to the Den, where the manager would be encouraging them and cheering them back. We would struggle in after them, terribly out of breath.

Although I was under contract, a sword of Damocles was hanging over me because I knew that at eighteen I could be called up for national service. If Millwall had seen me as being a potential first-class player, they would have given me an extended contract that would have paid me during my national service and ensured my return to the club. As it was, under the terms of my contract the deal with Millwall would be nullified if and when I was called to do national service. Even at that age I recognised that I wouldn't be another Tommy Lawton, one of the great England centre forwards, but I hoped that I could still make a decent living as a part-time footballer and a butcher.

The country was fighting on several fronts in 1952, in Malaya, Korea, Cyprus and Kenya, and national service was compulsory for all fit young men. We all had to register and have a medical, which I had passed as A1 fit. I told the briefing officer that I had just signed a contract with Millwall and, hearing about my training as a butcher, he told me that I would be ideal for the catering corps, based in Aldershot, a big football town. I was quite content with the set-up and was fully expecting to join the catering corps.

While waiting for my call-up I was playing in the pre-season and had a few games in the reserves. Sometimes I was simply listed on the team sheet as A. N. Other and, on walking on to the field, the announcer would give my name. In the training session we would often play the probables against the possibles to determine who would be selected to play in the squad.

During that time, I went on holiday to visit my uncles, aunts and cousins in Berwick-on-Tweed. I hadn't seen them since my childhood evacuation and my grandfather and grandmother had died since then. My uncle Adam played football now and again as a reserve for Berwick and he took me to watch a game. After the game I was approached by the manager, who had been told by Adam that I had just been signed by Millwall and that I was staying with my family for a couple of weeks. He suggested that if I wanted to get some practice in I could play for Berwick and, if this would cause me problems with Millwall under the terms of my arrangement with Millwall, I could play under another name. So I had three games for them in two weeks under my mother's maiden name, as Eddie Brown. They were in a lower league then; nowadays they are in the Scottish League Two and I still look out for their results with some affection.

After my holiday, two or three months passed with no word from the army so I was beginning to hope they had forgotten me. One Wednesday afternoon, however, having played in a reserve game against Leyton Orient, with a 2 o'clock kick off because we didn't have flood lights in those days, I got home and opened the door with the key that was hanging on a piece of string inside the letter box. My brother-in-law and sister were living with us at the time and he was home from Leadenhall Market after his early shift. He asked me about the game and I told him enthusiastically that Banger Forsyth, our trainer, had told me that I was starting to look like a real player.

With that, John handed me a brown envelope with 'On His Majesty's Service' in black letters, and said to me 'There you are. It's your call-up papers.' Inside was a letter telling me to report to Maidstone Barracks to the 1st Battalion of the Royal West Kent

Regiment. (Incidentally, I notice now that their cap badge with the 'rampant horse of Kent' is the one used on the uniforms in Dad's Army.)

It was just at the start of the football season so my first thought was that it was not great timing. I had never heard of the regiment but John said that it was the infantry and a fighting mob. 'That can't be right,' I told him. 'I'm going into the catering corps. Perhaps they are going to transfer me from there?'

A RUDE AWAKENING

At the beginning of August I reported to Maidstone, still firmly convinced that I was heading for the catering corps. I was in for a rude awakening. As we were dropped off by an army truck at the barracks, a loud-mouthed corporal was bawling and shouting obscenities. Years later I recognised the same behaviour watching the recruits being drilled in the film *An Officer and a Gentleman*.

That night we were taken to the stores and given our kit and bedding and were shown our barrack room. Within half an hour, which we spent trying to work out what we should be doing, the door flew open and a loud-mouth corporal about five-foot-eight, smaller than me, shouted out 'Buxton'.

'Yeh, that's me,' I shouted back.

He came straight up to me and shouted into my face, 'That's me? That's me? When I call your name, you say "Yes, corporal." You're one of the fucking privileged are you? You kick a fucking football so you think you're going to get special treatment. You report to the stores at fourteen hundred hours. You'll be playing against the brave boys who've just come back from Malaya. They're going to give you a game of football. Looking at you lot, we'll never win the fucking war with you.'

We played the game and were soundly beaten by the Malayan draft. Nevertheless, I was picked to play for the battalion in the first round of the Army Cup in Maidstone, which we won.

Our drill sergeant Palmer (Pedler Palmer to us) had also been a decent footballer. He came in and addressed us after we had got our football kit. He had come back from Malaya, having been shot in the throat so he had lost part of his vocal chords and talked in a strange voice. I couldn't resist the temptation to imitate him. The lads had been given the chore of scrubbing the barracks, so I was walking up and down barking out instructions in a comic voice like the drill sergeant's, when, unbeknown to me, Pedler Palmer silently slipped into the room and was standing behind me.

I whirled round as be roared out in his unique rasping voice, 'Buxton, you bastard. Report to my room at 6 a.m. tomorrow morning with my coffee, without fail.'

The lads were in fits of laughter that I had been caught out.

The following morning at 6 a.m. sharp I was at Pedler Palmer's door with his coffee. I went into the room where he seemed to be sound asleep. I wasn't sure if he heard me as he didn't react to a gentle cough so I walked over and touched his arm. Suddenly he shot up, instantly awake, jarring my arm and sending the coffee flying all over the walls. As he growled menacingly 'Don't ever touch me like that again,' I made a hasty getaway.

I thought I would need to keep out of his sight from then on but in fact he seemed to take a shine to me after that. He always gave me decent jobs and even invited me once to join him on a day out for a drink with his girlfriend. She had a friend with her and I had the feeling that he was trying to get me fixed up, but I didn't fancy her so nothing came of it.

After we finished our six weeks' initial training at Maidstone, we were transferred to Canterbury for ten weeks' advanced training in Stoughton Barracks in Canterbury.

It was then that I first came in contact with the Kray twins. They were both boxers for the Repton Boxing Club in Bethnal Green. They had been put into the Royal Fusiliers, so they knew they were to be sent to Korea where our troops were fighting the communists, as they were in Malaya. They didn't want to be in the army and they had no intention of doing any soldiering.

Because I was playing football for the army team I had a few privileges, as did members of the boxing team. I was assigned, along with a member of the military police who was a member of the boxing team, to guard the twins, who had been locked up in barracks because they refused to soldier and were awaiting a court martial. At that time they were still young men, the same age as me, so they seemed to me like just young tearaways from East London, but they were already gaining in notoriety. They were both quite small, about five foot eight, and their father Charlie was a small man too. I only learned later that during the Second World War he too had refused to soldier, so he had obviously influenced his sons, but Charlie told me at the time that their mother, Violet, didn't want them to fight. 'What she says goes,' he said.

The sergeant major, a tall man who looked like Lee Marvin, used to come by their cell and rattle his yard stick along the bars, goading them. The twins then went on hunger strike and refused to come out. They demanded to see the priest, who eventually turned up and went in and sat between them, hoping to be a calming influence. He was to be disappointed. During the conversation Ronnie picked up the slop bucket and tipped it over the priest's head, only one of many incidents during their stay in Canterbury, which culminated in them attacking a guard and escaping into the countryside, heading towards the city centre.

Once they were on the loose, our platoon was sent out to bring them back. We spread out in a line led by the sergeant major, who as usual was bawling and shouting instructions. As we moved towards the city, we came over a hill and the sergeant major spotted a figure in the distance. He shouted to the platoon 'That's one of them,' and sent us after him.

The boy took one look at us and took to his heels but he quickly realised that there was no escape and gave himself up. It turned out that he wasn't one of the Krays at all but was one of the lads in the catering corps, who had slipped out without permission and had thought he would be able to slip quietly back into the camp without being noticed. Instead, the poor unsuspecting boy had been confronted by the entire platoon and earned a seven-day stint confined to barracks doing jankers, as the official punishment for a minor breach of discipline was known as all the rotten jobs that no one else wants to do.

Meanwhile, the Krays had made their getaway. Ronnie was later caught in Canterbury and I understand that Reggie got all the way back to London before he was picked up by the local police.

Some years later when I was with Tottenham, after the army, I briefly met again with the Krays' father, Charlie, and his elder son, also called Charlie. It was in the Dirty Dick's pub in Bishopsgate. Ronnie and Reggie were already in prison by then, serving life sentences. I reminded Charlie Senior that we had met in Canterbury and we had a quiet chat, although I doubt that he remembered me as his memory seemed to be slipping by then and he was quite subdued. He died soon after.

Some months later I was having a meal in the Venus Steak House in Bethnal Green when the manager came over to me, leaned over and said quietly that someone wanted to talk to me at the bar. When it turned out to be Charlie Kray Jr. I wondered what he wanted with me but it turned out that he was very keen on football and just wanted to chat about the game. I told him that I was sorry to hear that his dad had died and he thanked me for having taken the time to chat to him on the previous occasion. He then gripped my arm and said, somewhat ominously, 'If there's anything I can do for you, and I do mean *anything*, just let me know.' That was the last time I ever saw him.

Back in Canterbury, I was told our next game was being played at Gillingham and I was called in by the drill sergeant who said, 'If we win this game, you won't go to Malaya or Korea.' It was thus to be a very important game for me.

We had to play the Military Police in Gillingham. For me the outcome was a disaster; not only did I miss a hat-full of chances in the first half, but we were beaten 1–0. As we came off the field, Keith (Spud) Spurgeon, who was also a semi-professional footballer, walked alongside me. He was a big lad, six foot four, and captain of the team.

I was already devastated at my performance but he didn't help. 'You can pack your fucking bags, 'cos you'll be on the next boat out,' he said.

Little did I know how right he was; the outcome of that one game was to determine my next two years and to have an impact on the rest of my life. After embarkation leave I was on the next boat out to Malaya.

I got my own back on Spud Spurgeon though. I was put on guard duty that weekend and should have stayed in the barracks after my stint but I slipped out into town and went downtown with a couple of other lads. While we were there I met Spud's then-girlfriend in a bar. She knew who I was so we had a few drinks and I was surprised when she invited me back home. I was a pretty inexperienced eighteen-year-old, so she taught me a thing or two that night.

I slipped back into barracks before roll call that morning, when we had a work-out under the watchful eye of Spud Spurgeon, the PT instructor. He said 'You've got over your game then. Did you do anything special at the weekend?'

I didn't give him any details but said with a broad smile, 'It was a really great weekend.'

He replied that it must have been a woman and I said with a knowing grin, 'You're absolutely right.'

But that was all – a gentleman never tells, especially when the guy concerned is six foot four and built like a heavyweight boxer.

Many years later I met Spud again when he recommended a player to me. I was at Tottenham and he was the football manager of a Greek side. Many years had passed and he seemed much diminished from my memories of the young man he had been. Sadly, he died not long after from a heart attack.

When we finished our training and were waiting to be sent to Malaya, we went home on embarkation leave but had only been there a couple of days when there was serious flooding around Kent. We were all called back and sent to the Isle of Sheppey to help the civilians fill sandbags and build barricades against the flood water. It was freezing cold and wet and we were not too happy being called back from our last leave.

I was in charge of my section and the civilian in charge of the council workers was supposed to work with us. He was an arrogant bastard who kept bragging that they were all on overtime, knowing that we were only getting our normal pay and missing our leave. One afternoon he went off with his crew and left us to fill the sandbags alone. They were a couple of hours late back, while we were left shovelling wet sand into bags using short shovels. When they returned and I challenged him about the time he had taken and that my lads hadn't had a break, he replied sarcastically, 'Mind your own business, soldier boy,' and swung dismissively away.

I was so incensed that I picked up my shovel and whacked him across the back of his shoulder, knocking him to the ground where he lay swearing at me. I stood over him and he made no attempt to get up because I would have whacked him again if he had come at me. My lads cheered and we all went off to have our break, leaving him on the ground and the rest of the civilians to continue with the sandbags. Nowadays, I probably wouldn't have been able to get away with it but they were different times – and we were shortly being sent off to war.

MALAYA BOUND

On my last night of leave before leaving for Malaya, I was at New Cross Palais with mates from Millwall. My brother Alf found me there and told me that my pregnant sister, Edie, had been rushed to hospital in Greenwich to have her baby. I jumped on a tram with my brother to see her but the battleaxe of a matron wouldn't let me meet the baby. In those days they were incredibly strict about only allowing one visitor so I had to leave without even seeing my new-born nephew.

In the morning, I took the 2 a.m. milk train to Maidstone where we were all marshalled and put onto troop trains down to Southampton to join the SS Orwell which would take us to Malaya. Only a few dockers were there to wave us off as we set off on what was the start of an adventure. I had never been further than Scotland before. We passed through the Mediterranean and docked at Port Said, where we got our first glimpse of a new exotic world, but we weren't allowed off the ship.

We went through the Suez Canal and the Red Sea and finally docked in Aden where we were let off the ship and taken to a nearby army barracks. Having left the cold January weather of England, the transition to the desert climate of Aden was an extreme one but it was good preparation for our arrival in Singapore a couple of weeks later.

From Singapore we were taken in armoured troop carriers through the Malayan Causeway into Johor Bahru and to our camp at Selangor, where we were issued with our jungle kit and weapons.

Mine was an American automatic M2 carbine, much lighter than the Lee Enfield rifles that we had trained with. I discovered that a magazine issued to me contained bullets that had been filed down by the soldier who had been issued with the carbine before me, but I didn't know at the time that this was intended to inflict more damage than a regular bullet. You learn fast in wartime.

Soon after my arrival in Malaya, I was sent out with Corporal Jeffcott to bring back the bodies of two bandits killed by the local police. The police lived in the local village and didn't want it known that they had killed the men, so word was put out that we had finished them off ourselves and we were sent with a driver and one of our Military Police to pick them up.

When we got to them, the bodies had been left overnight in the heat and were surrounded by flies and the stench of death. They were loaded onto the back of the truck, with labels on their toes, and were covered with a canvas. I was put between them, keeping guard to stop the villagers trying to lift the canvas to check who had been killed. As I sat in the truck, amid the stench of the corpses on either side, I realised that this was my initiation into jungle warfare.

My next mission seemed a simple one. The notorious Chinese terrorist leader Liew Kon Kim had recently been killed by the Suffolk Regiment and we were told that his mistress Ah Ying had taken over from him. Subsequently, I learned that she was reported killed at the same time as Liew Kon Kim but at the time we were told that we were being sent to take out Ah Ying, a pregnant but dangerous Chinese terrorist leader in the uprising in the colony during the early 1950s. It was Chinese New Year 1953 and the intelligence reports indicated that she was expected to be picking up supplies in a local village.

Three platoons of D company were briefed that we were to take her out. When she came into the village, the captain and 11 platoon were supposed to open up first; my platoon, 10, was positioned opposite him in case she made off in a different direction, he was to force her towards us. And 12 platoon was at the back to block off the last escape route.

We were in position and she was expected at first light; we waited and waited on high alert. A couple of hours passed with no sign of her and by that time we were waning. There was a curfew on the villagers during the night-time and this was nearly over. The mission would have to be aborted if she didn't appear before the curfew was lifted.

Just when we expected to be stood down and were thinking nothing was going to happen, there was a movement in the jungle and four figures stepped warily into the edge of the clearing. A young woman was at the front, dressed in black with a bandana around her head, a sub-machine gun strapped across her body and a belt of ammunition over her shoulders. She was looking guardedly from left to right and gesturing to the three heavyset men with her, who were also heavily armed. As they moved forward into the clearing, we could see four others spread out behind them.

We in 10 platoon were now fully alert; our safety catches were off to be ready for action and we were lying in wait with the terrorists in our sights, anticipating the signal to pick off the individuals as we had been briefed. My heart was pounding and the salty sweat was rolling from my forehead. We continued to wait.

The terrorists picked up the supplies and turned to head back into the jungle. 11 platoon should have opened up but still we waited. A few more seconds and the terrorists would be back in the safety of the trees. We couldn't wait for 11 platoon so I as acting corporal said 'Let's go,' and we opened fire.

I aimed at the woman but I must have missed her. Her reflexes were amazing and at the first sound she leapt into the jungle and was gone. Two of her escorts were killed but the rest escaped. There was no point in pursuing them as the gunfire had brought all the villagers out.

After lying in the jungle all night on full alert, eaten alive by mosquitos, failing to take out the leaders left us frustrated and disappointed, even though we had managed to take out two of the terrorists. We felt even more let down when 11 platoon admitted that they had simply relaxed when the terrorists hadn't arrived as expected and hadn't seen them when we had, so had done nothing.

In August 1953 my platoon had just finished a 'five-finger' patrol, where the platoon moves outwards in five directions to cover a wide area, scouring the area for the elusive Ah Ying and her gang, again without success. We made camp on a ridge where a small stream ran down to a pool where fish were swimming. Some of the lads boiled water to make a brew but I and a few others drank from the water in the stream and, seeing the fish, made the mistake of not using our purifying tablets.

At first light next morning, we moved out and were met by our escort at the eleventh milestone. Back at the base, after I had put in my report, I settled onto my bunk to read my mail from home. I started sweating profusely and then felt icy cold. I was aching all over and felt dog-tired but within an hour, I was told the CO wanted to talk to me. I dragged myself to my briefing and was told to take the platoon out again at first light to follow up the latest information on Ah Ying. I managed to crawl back to my bunk and that was the last thing I remember before waking up in a military hospital in Kuala Lumpur.

Apparently my temperature had soared to 105°F and I had been taken by military helicopter to the hospital where our doctors and American doctors, all officers in the Medical Corps, were investigating a similar outbreak of disease in Korea. They were calling it 'West Kent Fever'. I had to be given a lumbar puncture for which I was bent double, knees to my chest, biting into a twisted bed sheet, while the doctors spent fifteen minutes trying to get the needle into my spine. It was unbearably painful and had to be repeated the following day.

They didn't seem to give me much in the way of medication, just ice packs on my neck and groin to keep my temperature down, but the good food and attention from the Queen Alexandra nurses got me through it. A week later I was told that the disease was Leptospirosis, also known as Weil's disease, caused by rats' piss in the water that we had drunk on our last patrol and that a few soldiers had died of it. Four weeks later I was back on active duty but it took its toll and my lungs are still scarred today.

Sometime later we were again out on a routine patrol in an area where terrorist activity had been reported. We had already traversed most of the area with no sign of anything, so we were resigned to a fruitless search when suddenly our Iban tracker from the Sarawak Rangers, who was leading the way, fell to his knees. He had seen and smelled something in the air. As we moved quietly forward we hit a clearing where four or five bandits were smoking and cooking on an open fire. They spotted us; in a panic they let off a few shots and started to run. We quickly opened up and rushed the clearing. Suddenly I felt a searing pain across my left side. I lost my footing hitting the ground where I lay gasping for breath.

It was all over in minutes with one bandit wounded and one captured. When transport arrived to pick us up, I found that I had a burn mark that was bleeding and what turned out to be a cracked rib. I think whoever let that gun off must have been someone behind me getting excited. Nowadays they call it 'friendly fire' but it didn't seem that friendly at the time. And later in another incident I got caught in an ambush and suffered perforated eardrums, leaving me with impaired hearing on one side. No one comes away from warfare totally unscathed.

In December 1953, all of us in 10 platoon, along with other platoons, were sent out on a routine four-day patrol to a bandit camp that had been spotted deep in the jungle. We were carrying four days' rations plus our equipment, so it was heavy going through swampy terrain, rife with mosquitos and leeches. Whenever we had the chance to stop, we spent the time burning the leeches off our bodies, otherwise they would drain the blood and attract even more mosquitos.

When we arrived at the camp it had been abandoned. The other platoons converged on the area, where we found that the bandits must have vacated in a hurry because they had left behind a lot of valuable intelligence about the location of similar camps in the surrounding area, which we reported back to HQ. We were now told that this was to be part of a bigger operation, named Operation Blick after Colonel H B H (Blick) Waring.

We were told to hold the camp while the other platoons were despatched elsewhere. By Christmas Eve our rations had run out, except for a few biscuits and some curry powder and we were told that an airdrop of supplies was impossible because of the density of the jungle. On Christmas Day, one of the Iban trackers went out on his own and came back with an anteater that he had killed and bled in accordance with his religion.

We were still on alert for surprise attacks by bandits while we watched the Iban tracker stewing the anteater in a pot. He then went to a tree, opened up the bark to reveal a nest of red ants, grabbed a handful of ants and crushed them and dropped them in the pot. The other Iban tracker was making encouraging noises as roots and leaves were added so we gave him our curry powder, which he enthusiastically added to the mix. The smell was pretty awful as the officers dished out the food, but we were hungry and it went down a treat. As Christmas Day feasts go, 1953 was a meal I will never forget.

On Boxing Day morning we were told that HQ Company had been sent out from base on a forced march with double rations to reach us that evening. We clapped and cheered when they arrived but they were completely exhausted after completing in two days a march that would normally take four. The weight of the supplies had cut into their shoulders and they were covered in leeches and had to be treated by the medics. Even so, we were never so glad to see anyone as those lads arriving in the camp.

When we eventually got back to our base camp we were told that our company, D Company, had killed 27 bandits and that the Regiment had totalled 100. The officer was a big cricket man and he announced to the radio operator that 'We have reached our century.' The radio operator thought initially that he was talking about the score in the England cricket game, but that type of wry humour was one way of getting through the war. The tally was even displayed on a cricket-style score board at HQ.

After Operation Blick, at the start of 1954 the regiment was told that we had done our tour of duty and were due to sail home in April, so during those last few months we just expected to do routine patrols.

We then received information about a bandit camp that had been spotted in the Salangor region, again near the Batu caves. So 10 platoon was sent out into the jungle with an Iban tracker to help us locate them. We started to climb, to have a tactical advantage, but it was stiflingly hot, moving uphill laden with our equipment.

We reached the top of one of the ridges and stopped for a breather in the high humidity. As we started to climb again, it began raining heavily as we were now coming into the monsoon season. The tracker came back and excitedly pointed to footprints on the level ground where the rain was filling the footprints and indicating that the bandits were ahead of us on the higher level. Clearly, this would put us at a disadvantage as the bandits had the higher ground; I feared we were walking into an ambush.

The tracker was keen to pursue the bandits but, as his tracking task was complete, he now fell back to give us the lead. The rain was relentless. In all my time in the army I can honestly say that

I had never felt fear but I had a bad feeling about this situation. I always listen to my gut instincts so I made the decision to turn back, which was welcomed by the rest of the men. Clearly, they thought it didn't make sense to take foolhardy risks when we were so close to getting home. Back at base I reported that we had found traces of the enemy but, given their tactical advantage, had decided not to pursue them.

Within weeks the Gurkhas arrived to relieve the regiment and we were able to relax and get ready to go home as our time in Malaya was coming to an end. Although I was looking forward to returning to the UK, I knew that I would miss the buzz of army life. I had travelled out as an eighteen-year-old novice knowing nothing about life outside our small world in South London, had spent two years on constant alert in a war zone and had men reporting to me in life-threatening situations. It had proved to be a life-changing experience and now that we would be coming home as seasoned jungle fighters, I had some feelings of uncertainty and trepidation about what the future would hold for me on my return.

LIFE ON CIVVY STREET

When we arrived back from Malaya the regiment was given the freedom of Canterbury and Maidstone. As we arrived back in Maidstone barracks to wait for demob, a batch of recruits was being drafted in at the barracks. Although they had different corporals and sergeants drilling them, I had a sense of déjà-vu seeing ourselves as we had been when we arrived as raw conscripts. We heard the same words: 'Look at these brave boys back from Malaya. You'll never be as good as these boys coming back. You'll probably not make it back alive.' Different officers, different soldiers, but the same routine that we heard on our arrival two years previously.

Back on civvy street, I returned to Morris's in Leadenhall Market as a trainee butcher as it was a condition that employers had to take back those men who had been away on National Service. I was still keen to play football but the leptospirosis I suffered in Malaya had impaired my breathing, so I didn't have quite the pace I had had before. It wasn't a surprise when Ron Gray at Millwall told me that he couldn't take me on under contract. However, he did say that I could play if they were short so I returned to Millwall as a non-contract player. I used to turn up at reserve games and got the odd game only for expenses which helped me to get back some sort of normality.

Apart from occasional games with Millwall, I was playing Sunday football with a team called Norwood Celtic. In a cup tie, I had just gone by our opponents' centre-half when a tackle came in on me and I smashed into the goalkeeper and broke my collar bone. Nowadays I would probably have been sent off for leaving my foot in on the goalkeeper but times were different back then. As it was, I was sent to the hospital, but they didn't strap up my arm and shoulder as they would now so to this day I have a protruding collar bone.

While at Millwall, I had cleaned boots for Jackie Fisher and his brother George. Jackie had moved to Ramsgate together with a full back called Mike Snowball. I was at New Cross Palais one Saturday night when I met up again with Jackie, who took me aside and told me he would have a word with the manager at Ramsgate for me to come down and have a try-out.

With that I went down to pre-season training and did all right so they offered me a 'pay if you play plus expenses' arrangement. I was hopeful that I was back on track.

In one of the early games of the season I had a decent game against Gravesend. Playing up front, I scored a couple of goals and was feeling good. As I was leaving the ground to catch a train home I was approached by a Chelsea scout called Dickie Foss, who said that my brother-in-law, John, had told him about me (I have no idea where they had met), so he had come to the game and liked what he saw.

He said he would arrange for me to have a few games in Chelsea's Metropolitan League – non-contract again with expenses and a match fee. So my association with Chelsea began. I had about half a dozen games, mainly around the Surrey area – Weybridge and Leatherhead – and I did all right. Chelsea had a big squad, even in those days. They had won the League in the 1954–55 season and Ted Drake was the manager, a real gentleman. Ted and his mate Tom Smith were into dog racing and horse racing so we often got tips for both animals, some of which came off.

By April, near the end of the season, Ted Drake said he wanted to see me. I was full of hope but came down to earth with a bump when he said I had done well but he couldn't offer me anything as they had a couple of younger players who were forcing their way through into the first team. Both of them went on to become internationals and superstars – Jimmy Greaves and Bobby Smith.

Ted Drake was being kind in letting me down gently because I wasn't in their class and, in all honesty, I knew from then on that the big time wasn't going to come to me as a player.

I celebrated my twenty-first birthday playing in a reserve game and afterwards going out with a few of the lads to New Cross Palais. It was here that we met up with a group of girls and invited them all back to my mum's house. We all agreed to meet the following week at the Marquis of Granby pub near Deptford Town Hall. I chatted to one of the girls, Joyce, and when she told me that she had to go home to Lewisham on the tram, like a gentleman I offered to take her home. I then asked her if she would like to go to the pictures the following week.

The next week came and I had come straight from the dog track at Catford, so had just enough money, about one shilling and six pence each, to get into the cinema, the Gaumont Palace in Lewisham. As we were going in, we bumped into Henry Cooper and his brother George and had a chat with them. I used to do a bit of boxing as a schoolboy when I had represented the district in regional tournaments and knew Henry and George from Manor Place Baths, where my brother-in-law used to box as a sparring partner to some of the fighters. Joyce seemed a bit impressed that I knew Henry Cooper so she invited me home for a coffee.

As we walked to her house down one of the streets full of rambling old houses in Lewisham next to the River Quaggy, we stopped by a house with an enormous hammer and sickle painted on the fence. Everyone knows I am quite right wing politically, so seeing this I didn't mince my words about 'damned communists'. When Joyce then told me that this was her house and her father was a communist this did not seem to bode well for our blossoming relationship as I just knew her father and I were not going to see eye to eye. Despite this, Joyce and I married when I was twenty-three and moved in to live on the top floor of her father's council house.

Life with the in-laws had its ups and downs and, after a while, I was getting restless. Then Joyce fell pregnant. I wanted to move out of the house and, as luck would have it, Lewisham Council decided that the row of old houses was to be knocked down and we would soon be rehoused.

In those days having babies at home was not unusual and an old midwife was appointed to attend the birth. She was a real Hattie Jacques-type character, a large buxom woman, but with a limp and so accordingly nicknamed 'Limp Along Lisa'. Joyce was having a terrible time, being in labour for nearly two days when Limp Along Lisa decided that a doctor should be called. She made me jump into my car to drive straight to the doctor's house, because we didn't have phones or mobiles back then.

Vince had been expected to arrive on Joyce's twenty-first birthday, 29th January, but he finally arrived three days later on 1st February 1960. When he was eventually delivered, Limp Along Lisa brought him down to my mother-in-law's on the ground floor. I took one look at him and thought 'Christ, he looks like a Martian!' as his head had a prominent point at the top.

I looked at the midwife in horror. She saw my reaction and promptly shoved him into my arms and shouted, 'There's nothing wrong with him. His head will be normal in a few days. He's your son.' There were a few tears of joy from my mother-in-law, Dolly, and Joyce's sister, Diane. The midwife was of course right and Vince's head soon returned to normal.

Soon after, the council arranged for us to move to a nice place in Sydenham, a new block of council flats called Peak Hill. Two years later our second son, John, was born, again at home. This time a doctor and a young nurse were on hand when he came into the world, just after midnight on the morning of 11th May. Dolly took hold of my hand and said 'Happy Birthday'. I had forgotten that it was my birthday and it seemed such a coincidence that Vince had been expected to arrive on Joyce's birthday and now John had arrived on mine. I took that to be a good omen.

Around that time I left Morris's and took a job as a meat buyer at Dewhursts, a big meat chain. The main reason for the move was that they were in Bishopsgate in the City and closed on Saturday, which suited me very well as I was able to relax on Saturdays, not having to rush from work to get to wherever we were playing a game. I had been determined to leave council housing so by now I had saved enough money to put down a deposit on our own home, a nice place around the corner in Whittell Gardens, which we bought for £4000.

Once we had moved in, I had an extension built and put in a butcher's block, a cabinet freezer and a mincing machine so that I could run a butcher's from home, buying meat from Smithfield and Leadenhall markets and supplying friends and neighbours. I even served the staff and players at Millwall. On Fridays and Saturdays, while I was out playing, Joyce would label the orders and price them up and would serve the neighbours who came knocking for their meat. At times they would be queuing in the passage waiting to be served.

My football-playing life was now nearing its end. I had been playing at Bexley Heath and Welling with Peter Payne, my brother-in-law who was married to Joyce's sister, Diane. Peter had been a pro at Leyton Orient and finished his career at Bexley (now Welling United). Then I got a chance to go to Tonbridge.

Harry Haslam was the manager there, a great character. When I drove to see him I was driving a Ford Capri, white with a black vinyl roof, quite a car in those days.

When Harry saw me get out of the car, he asked me an odd question: 'How many people could you get in it?'

'Four others and me,' I said.

He then asked me how old I was and, although I was actually in my early thirties, I said 'twenty-nine', because in those days hardly anyone got past that age at that level. In the Tonbridge side Harry had Malcolm Macdonald, Johnny Roach and Gus Simmons. Of course, Macdonald, who was playing as a full back in those days, finished up as a goal-scoring icon at Newcastle United.

Harry looked at me and said, 'I'll give you a year, but I've got a proposition for you. You can pick up some of the lads in your car and I'll give you extra,' (which amounted to about £15). I was never a regular, but no matter. At the end of the season I reckoned Harry owned me about £40 so I went to see him. He offered me another season but I had had enough as Harry had hardly played me and I had done enough chauffeuring. Later, Harry took over at Fulham and I saw him there. He still owed me the £40 but when I asked him for it he said 'You've got plenty.' Little did he know how tight money was for me at the time.

Although I hadn't played much for Harry, he seemed to like talking match tactics with me as we used to discuss the game and shifting players and I enjoyed that side of the game. So I was ready to move towards coaching, where my future seemed to lie.

SABOTAGE TED

I took coaching badges in the late sixties and seventies and in those days it was very different and much simpler than the way it is now. All you took in those days were the prelim and the full badges and that was it. That took about two or three years and you could still act as a coach all the while.

It was while I was taking my badges that I met Fred Callaghan on the coaching course on the first prelim and we've been best mates ever since. He was ten years younger than me and we teamed up on the badges under the coaches, Bobby Robson, Mike Kelly and Bobby Houghton. Fred and I paired up when we had to do training sessions and impress the coaches. In those days ex-professionals, who were planning to become coaches with football clubs, and schoolteachers, who were planning to become football coaches in schools, were mixed. They don't do that nowadays – you're separated.

The first incident came when I had to do a session for a schoolteacher, who had apparently failed a couple of times and was coming back for his third attempt to qualify to coach in schools. He chose Fred and me to take part in the session, which was called jockeying, in which the defender had to show the winger the line, not show him any tackles, just show the line and put him onto your partner. What the fellow didn't tell me was that I was not supposed to tackle, which I considered one of my strong points. It always seemed to me that if I had a chance of getting the ball, I should go for it. If he had explained that I wasn't supposed to tackle, I would have played as he wanted and it would have gone differently.

I was partnered with Fred. Where I should have been jockeying the young player that he had put against us, I put in a tackle instead and the young lad flew about three feet in the air. The schoolteacher was now standing on one side, jumping up and down trying to remonstrate with me, telling me that I was not to tackle and was just to show him the line. I was arguing with him saying that if I could tackle him, I would. So with that he changed me and Fred around, which I understood meant that I was now free to tackle.

Fred was to do the jockeying and I was the back-up man. Fred was jockeying the young player and he got half a yard past Fred when I came in and, once again, slung in a tackle. I went through him and Fred, the boy went down and all three of us ended in a heap. The schoolteacher was livid, shouting and bawling. Micky Kelly and Bobby Robson, who were supposed to be assessing the schoolteacher's performance, were laughing their heads off. With that the schoolteacher didn't get his coaching badge – he failed because he hadn't coached the situation properly – and as a result I got a reputation with everyone calling me 'Sabotage Ted.' Fred and I went on to finish our courses.

We had a similar incident at a later session with a fellow called Jimmy Rose, who was taking his coaching prelim badge for the fourth time – he said that if he didn't get his badge that time he would pack it in.

Jimmy Rose used Fred and me on his session to try to help to get him through his badge. It was a session on crossing and shooting, which didn't go well for him, and Fred and I started arguing with him, telling him what he should have done. Unfortunately, this meant he didn't get through again so my Sabotage Ted moniker continued.

Later on in the seventies, Jimmy Rose went on to own Dulwich Hamlet football club, a team I had played for as a kid. When I was looking for a coaching job, he phoned me up and asked if I wanted to work with him at Dulwich Hamlet, a job which I took. The pre-season and the start of the season went well. We were four games into the season unbeaten when I got a phone call from him on a Monday morning after we had won the previous Saturday game and he promptly told me that I'd got the sack. So when I asked why, he said, 'I don't think the players are getting on with you.'

I said, 'Are you fucking sure? Ask them.'

He just said, 'I have and I'm taking over the team myself.' So I take it that he had never forgotten his coaching session with me and Fred and it was a bit of payback time for him.

Having been fired, I told him that he owed me two weeks' pay. He owned a pub in Deptford called the Star and Garter so I went down there and got my money, which wasn't a lot – I think it was about 40 quid at the time. He offered me a drink so I had a glass of wine with him and he said, 'I think you'll do all right at some time but I think you let the players get away with too much.'

So that was the end of that – my first experience of being sacked, which at the time seemed to carry a stigma but years later became just a routine part of life for any football manager or coach.

Soon after I had got my coaching badges, Fred phoned me up and said Pat O'Connell, an old team mate of his at Fulham, had taken over as manager at Epsom and Ewell and he wanted somebody to help him because the club had been thrown out of the Athenian League. I went to meet Pat and got on well with him. He said, 'I'm short of players but Ray Bloye, the chairman of Crystal Palace, has put some money into Epsom and Ewell and put one of his directors in charge as chairman.'

I was still playing in non-league on a Sunday and, apart from my butchery business, I had also got a couple of nights' work with the local council, coaching and fitness training for local footballers, which helped to pay a few bills. The only trouble was that I was out most nights of the week and this did nothing for my marriage.

Joyce was and is a great lady. We're now great friends and the whole family is reunited but I don't think I was ever a very good husband and by that time I had met someone else and had been playing away. She was a friend of Joyce's and they spent time together with her two kids who were more or less the same age as my two, Vince and John.

We had known one another for about a year after Joyce and I had moved into a flat in Peak Hill in Sydenham. It was a nice area and we started spending a lot of time together as families. Joyce had started a catalogue business and June was involved with her in the venture. I had been busy because now I was playing part-time, training Tuesday and Thursday nights and spent quite a bit of time away from the family. Then one night I was sitting at home with the boys watching television, as Joyce had gone out with my sister for the night. The doorbell rang and June asked if Joyce was in as she had some money to pay her for the catalogue.

I said that she had gone out for the evening so she said, 'Can you give her this money?' She followed that up with the immortal words which gave me a jolt: 'I haven't seen you for a long time. I thought you didn't love me anymore.' Something stirred me up a bit and that was the start of a relationship that was to last a few years.

At the end of the season, both families had booked a holiday together at a cottage in the Kent countryside. Not surprisingly, the tension between us all was palpable and both of our partners knew something was going on. June decided that she had to do something about our relationship and decided to tell her husband about us. All hell broke loose. I bundled the boys and Joyce into the car and drove into the night and back home but it was then, after seventeen years of marriage, I decided to move out.

I had met a Polish couple through business who had a delicatessen in Clapham. They had a big house in Herne Hill in South London and rented out the top flat in the house and so, as I had decided to leave home, I moved into the flat. They were a lovely couple, Mr and Mrs Gorlow, who had been released from Russian concentration camps in Poland and had come to England to start their own business. They had apparently gone through hell in the camps – they never had any children and Mr Gorlow was always suffering with his health. It was years later after I had gone to America with the Tampa Bay Rowdies that I came home and tried to find out where they were. Obviously, the house had been sold.

He had died and she was in an old people's home somewhere in Surrey. I tracked her down and went to the home. It was quite emotional as she was so pleased to see me. I don't think she had anyone else around to visit her. I promised I would go down to see her again as soon as I had time, but unfortunately the next time I phoned to see if she was OK, I was told she had died. It was the end of an era but I will always appreciate what those two did for me as I think they looked on me as a bit of a son and they helped me through a difficult time.

At Epsom and Ewell we started off the league and Pat and I even had to turn out for the team for some games. We were looking at all the Sunday clubs for potential players and eventually picked up two black players, Trevor Lee and Phil Walker, as we started the season. We had a bit of a think about the opposition because we were going into the FA Vase, and it was the first season after the FA Vase took over from the FA Amateur Cup, so now money was being paid to players.

We took Trevor and Phil for £7 per week (I think they were playing for Cobham at the time). We started off the season very well. The reserves were doing well and then we went into the FA Vase and started to get through the stages of the competition. We got through the first round against a lesser team but then we got drawn against teams I, as a Londoner, had never heard of – up and around Peterborough, Brigtown and all these sort of places.

Neither Pat nor I knew much about them or the leagues they were playing in so I said to Pat, 'Listen. What we've got to do is go and look at these clubs during the week when they've got games so that we can see how well they're playing.'

Those regular visits to watch games helped to build my awareness of our opponents' strengths and weaknesses and I started to realise that I could handle the tactical side of the game. I drafted out reports and we relayed these to our players. We started playing our reserves in training in the way the opposition would play in the FA Vase games. It ended up as a terrific season for the club – we won the league; the reserves won their league and their league cups and we got to the FA Vase final V against Hoddesdon – the first time the FA Vase was played at Wembley.

It was then that I had a little falling-out with Pat on the selection of the Wembley team when he decided to put himself into the squad. He had finished playing but, because the game was at Wembley, he just wanted to play in the match. I disagreed with that because the boys who had got through were starting out and deserved to play. Pat put himself on the bench but I knew that, sooner or later, he would go on and that's exactly what he did. I had watched Hoddesdon in the previous mid-week game and their centre forward had a broken cheek bone. He had missed a couple of games as a result but was determined to play at Wembley. I told our centre half, a boy called Warby, to get into the centre forward early and just give him a little nudge on his cheek and stop him playing, but Warby was a gentle giant and never went near him. The boy scored two goals and we lost 2–1 but we'd had a great season.

After Epsom and Ewell I had my short, ill-fated stint at Dulwich Hamlet, which was mentioned earlier.

COACHING AND CURRIES

My eldest boy Vince was fifteen when he was taken on at Millwall as a schoolboy. When Vince signed, I went down to talk to Gordon Jago, the manager at the time. Gordon had obviously been following the success of Epsom and Ewell, as our achievements were in the local paper. Gordon asked me what I was going to do football-wise because at that time I was still running my butchery business at Leadenhall and Smithfield markets.

I was doing all right with the meat business but football was still what I wanted to focus my life on. Gordon said, 'I could do with someone here to help on a Tuesday and Thursday night training the kids.'

So he offered me a small wage for those two nights and I had been quite enjoying it when he phoned me at home one night and asked me if I would go down and have a chat. I really didn't know what to make of it, wondering whether I was about to get the elbow. He surprised me when he sat me down and asked if I would come and work with the first team with him and with Theo Foley, an ex-Irish international who had played for Charlton.

Now, apart from training the kids on Tuesday and Thursday, I was with the first team and doing what I could with the time I had.

At that point I was getting up at 3.30 in the morning, getting into Smithfield Market and buying what meat I needed for the restaurants that I was supplying in the area. I got in with Fred Lingham, a fellow who had a butcher's shop in Forest Hill who was a 'bummaree' (porter) in Smithfield, and he allowed me to work from his shop. I dumped my meat there in order to get down to Millwall by 9.30 a.m. to train till about 12.30 p.m. with the team, and then got back to Fred's shop. There I would get the meat ready for several restaurants – that mostly wanted loins of pork and pieces of chicken. Indian restaurants were just starting to open in London so I was supplying meat for the curry shops. A couple of steak houses took whatever meat I had, such as sirloins and loins of pork, and they normally cut their own portions so I was able to deliver to them in bulk. Then I used to collect my money from them in the evening. So it was a long day.

Most of the restaurants and steak houses paid on time, but I had a problem with the Indian restaurants as they wanted to have their meat and pay a week later, so they were always behind.

I went round to one Indian restaurant that was a particularly bad payer. After weeks chasing my money, I showed up one evening when the owner had a few people in the restaurant in Camberwell New Road. I had decided that I wouldn't supply him anymore but I wanted my money. I got him into his little room at the back of the restaurant and said 'Are you going to pay me tonight?'

'Next week, next week,' he said, so I pinned him up against the wall and told him I had a couple of mates outside waiting for me. 'If I don't get my fucking money now, you'll have no shop left tonight. I'm going to go outside to talk to my friends and I'll be back in ten minutes. If the money's not there, the restaurant won't be either.'

I went off, waited around the corner, because of course it was all bluff and I had no mates with me, and when I went back in the money was handed over with an elastic band round it. As I walked out of the shop, the cheeky bastard shouted out, 'What about next week's order?' You can imagine what I shouted back.

It was at that time that Fred Lingham asked me if I would go into business with him because of my connections with the restaurants. I agreed because that meant he would collect the meat while I could go to Millwall and do what I wanted in the afternoons after the football.

At Millwall, Gordon, with Theo Foley, was doing most of the coaching at the time. Gordon would take a step back and let Theo take the actual daily coaching but after about two weeks he called me in and asked if I would like to do a bit with Theo. I started to get to know the players and a lot of banter started between us because the players seemed to respond to me. That must have got back to Gordon because he started to come out and watch the training.

Gordon also got more directly involved in the tactical side of the game and started to involve me more. I had been doing the assessments for the opponents and Gordon used to bring down my reports to the training ground and go through them with me. He would then set out the training session with the young reserves and the youth team as the opposition and would encourage me to put forward my suggestions about how we should play. He told me later that he thought the players responded very well.

Gordon then asked me what I thought of the squad. I said, 'Well, there are two players I had at Epsom and Ewell that could be good squad players and probably better than what we've got in certain positions.'

At that time there was a lot of racism in South London, as there was in much of the country. Gordon said he would send two of his scouts to watch the two lads, Trevor Lee and Phil Walker, playing at Epsom. After the scouts had seen them, Gordon phoned me on a Sunday morning and said he had sent Derek Healy, who was his chief scout at the time, and Bob Pearson, who was a part-time scout, and their report about the two lads was not particularly favourable.

I was not only disappointed, I was absolutely livid because I disagreed. I knew the lads and had worked with them. We had won the league and the cup and gone to Wembley for the first FA Vase final. I went in on the following Monday morning after my stint at Smithfield and sat down with Gordon. I said, 'I certainly don't agree with their report. Gordon, it's going to cost you nothing to get them in to have a look at for a week. I can arrange that. If they don't work out, what have you lost? If it does work out, it'll cost you £2000. If after a period you don't think they're good enough, I'll give you back your two grand.' I don't know how I was going to give him that as I didn't even have two bob.

Somewhat reluctantly, Gordon brought them in and the season went quite well. With the next season coming up, we started off reasonably well and then fell away and lost a couple of games. When Gordon phoned me one day, the two lads had been doing quite well in the reserves and looked good in training. I think we were playing Notts County when Gordon sat me down and said, 'I've read your reports on Notts County. I think I'll play Phil Walker down the left-hand side because that's where you think we can get at Notts County.'

This was tricky. I said to Gordon, 'If you're going to play one, pick both of them. Put Trevor up front.'

'Ted, how can I do that?' he asked. 'Two black boys from non-league playing against this crowd down here? If it doesn't come off, I'll get slaughtered.'

I said, 'Gordon, trust me. They won't let you down.' It was a tight game. We won 1–0. Phil Walker slaughtered the full back half way through the second half and got in a great cross. Trevor Lee got across his marker and headed a great goal. The 8000-strong crowd went mad. We had three points in the bag and the lads went off to a standing ovation. It was quite emotional, really – certainly for me. It also made me realise that you've got to stick to your guns, say what you think and do what's right, whatever others think.

Millwall was going for promotion on our run of sixteen games undefeated. We were playing Crystal Palace, and Peter Taylor was their left winger. They were also going for promotion so we couldn't afford to be beaten. The game was going into a 0–0 draw when the ball went out for a throw-on and landed in our dugout between me and Theo Foley. Theo, being very volatile, picked it up and threw the ball down the touch line before Peter Taylor could pick it up and throw it in. Taylor looked at both of us, me and Theo, and told us both to 'Fuck off'.

To which I said, 'You're useless, you fat bastard.' Taylor was becoming very agitated. Five minutes later, the referee had perhaps got very irritated with both me and Theo for the little outburst, as he awarded Palace a penalty, which Taylor was going to take. As Taylor walked to the penalty spot, he looked over to us with a very smug expression. I mouthed again, 'You fat bastard'. He promptly missed the penalty. It was one of the worst penalties I've ever seen – high and wide – so the game finished in a draw.

The season went well after that. We went the last sixteen games undefeated. Ray Goddard, our goalkeeper (God bless him, he's dead now), was making world-class saves every game and we reached the final stage at which we had to win our last two games to get promoted. We won the first one and then had to go up to Swindon for the last game.

In between games, Gordon had called in a psychologist called Romark, who got the players together. I don't know what he did but he psyched them up. He picked out Trevor Lee and Phil Walker, to prove to the rest of the players what power he had. He put Trevor to sleep once and he got Phil to lie with his head on one chair and his feet on another chair, as stiff as a board in between them, and then woke him up. It was unbelievable.

We still hadn't been beaten so Gordon had it in mind that we should keep Romark on. In the game before our match at Swindon, Romark had heard that somebody in the crowd had been banging a drum all through the game. He said to Gordon that we must have that man to get the team psyched up for the Swindon game. So with the help of the local media they tracked down the bloke.

Gordon put him out on the pitch at the Old Den before we left for Swindon. He said, 'Ted, get the players out of the coach and onto the pitch. We've got this guy banging the drum.'

Romark was out there as well. I went to the lads and said, 'You've got to go and hear this guy banging the drum for Romark.'

They looked to me in amazement. A chorus of voices went, 'Are you fucking sure?'

'Well that's what he wants,' I replied.

With that, Terry Brisley and Ray Goddard said in tandem, 'Bollocks. We're sitting here.'

So I went straight out to report back to Gordon and I couldn't stop laughing. Gordon, very seriously, said, 'What's happened?'

I said their answer is, 'Bollocks. They're not coming out.'

So still very serious, Romark whispered something in Gordon's ear. He said, 'Right. We'll take the drum to them. We'll take the drummer on the coach with us.'

I said, 'Gordon, you can't do that. Let him go up by car with someone and bang it out at Swindon.'

'Good idea,' he said.

Off we went to Swindon. When we got there we were all in the dressing room sharing our normal banter and talking match tactics, pinning up the set plays and getting all the players around to familiarise them with it. We walked out on the ground to have a look at the pitch, deciding what boots the players were going to wear, when we heard that the geezer with the drum wasn't allowed in the ground. So he stood outside the ground banging this drum and nearly got arrested.

I don't know what happened to Romark but we had to concentrate on the game because we had more problems. Our captain and centre half, Barry Kitchener, who was a colossus for the club and the team, had broken a toe in his left foot and he was a left-sided player. He was in agony but wanted to play. The only way he would get through was with injections. The club doctor came in half an hour before the warm-up, sat with the physio, opened up Barry's toes in between the broken one and the others.

I can remember Barry hanging on to the hangers where the clothes were above his head, while the doctor stuck this needle between his toes. That first needle looked huge. The expression on Barry's face was sheer agony. When that first one went in there was a sigh of relief until the doctor said, 'You must have another one.'

He opened up his other two toes. Barry put his arm round my shoulders and said 'Fuck this. Will it work, Doc?'

The doctor just said, 'We'll see.'

In went the needle and Barry looked relieved but it was clearly absolute agony for a while. Barry was the type that you would want in the trenches with you. That's why I signed him and took him to Tampa Bay Rowdies a couple of years later. He was a winner and we won that Swindon game 2–0. It took Barry a week to recover from that, but we had won our promotion.

In those years I had managed to keep the butchery business going and was now supplying some of the players and the staff with their weekend meat. At that time a young blonde lady lived opposite the shop I shared with Fred Lingham. She had a large six-bedroom house, but was divorced with three young daughters and had her mum and dad living with them as well so she was struggling to make ends meet. She was doing two or three jobs, even cleaning. I happened to mention one day that Millwall was looking for a place to lodge young players coming in from outlying districts. I thought it would be a good idea if she could put them up and feed them and we would give her a fee for board and lodgings. When I put this to Gordon Jago he spoke to the chairman and they thought it was a great idea. Hence, the relationship that Linda Doyle, for it was she, built up with Millwall as the most glamorous landlady the players said they had ever seen. I never saw Linda without make up, always stunning, as she just happened to look like a film star.

When we signed Bryan Hamilton, an Irish international from Everton who had also played for Ipswich, he needed time to find a place of his own with his wife and family so I made arrangements for him to stay with Linda. When his wife came down to see where he was staying I think she was not best pleased to meet the attractive landlady and hurried to find a place of their own. Even the young players who lodged there never wanted to move. Linda and I remained friends and she went off and married someone quite high up in the police force, who was a member of their shooting team, I understand. Now she lives with him in Eastbourne.

UNCLE SAM CALLS

After another couple of decent seasons, Gordon was approached in 1977–78 by Tampa Bay Rowdies to take over as coach. He was going to Florida to negotiate and asked me if I would go with him, which meant giving up my various roles in the UK. He had to have an answer because, if I didn't go, he would have to find someone else. I gathered that he hadn't mentioned it to Theo Foley, his number two, probably thinking he wouldn't want to relocate to the States, but if I had turned him down, he might have approached him. I, on the other hand, was footloose and fancy free. Gordon is interested in management psychology and he had apparently had someone in to assess all the staff to judge what their leadership capabilities would be. At the time I didn't know that that included me and it wasn't until sometime later that I was told that I was the only one who was deemed to have leadership potential. Perhaps my days in Malaya had taught me that much.

After speaking to Vince and John and my sister and brother-in-law, I decided to pack my bags and go. After meeting Gordon and the Tampa Bay representatives in London, they offered me a two year contract, plus a car and an apartment in Tampa. I would earn a lot more than working part-time on coaching and running my butchery business in the UK. It also sounded exotic and so it proved to be. It was a sensational start to the big time and to this day I tell young coaches at the London Coaches Dinner and other similar events that it is never too late if you stand by your principles and are honest with people. Anything can happen. For me it exceeded all my expectations.

After Gordon left for America, it was some time before I was due to follow him. Theo Foley had taken over as manager at Millwall with me helping out with coaching and scouting. Theo then left to join up with George Graham, so Millwall decided to bring in another manager, George Petchey, who was ex-Brighton and Crystal Palace. The first day that George came into Millwall, a few of the players, who had played with him before, weren't too happy.

On his first day we were sitting waiting for him to show up. We had all changed and were ready to go out training. Jack Blackman, the old kitman, had set the dressing room out ready for the new manager but when George walked in, it was obvious that Jack, for whatever reason, had given him the worst tracksuit I had ever seen. It was too big for him and looked a bit discoloured. Knowing Jack Blackman as well as I did, I knew he hoarded everything. I remember once previously we had needed new training equipment and found twenty years of brand-new stuff still in its cellophane in his cupboards. So it was obvious he hadn't wanted to give George any new stuff.

As George wheeled in, there was deadly silence in the dressing room. He looked around and saw that Terry Brisley and Ray Goddard hadn't changed – they were still in their day clothes. George narrowed his eyes; he obviously already knew them as they were his former players.

'Are you both injured?' he asked.

'No, we don't want to fucking play for you,' they replied in unison.

With that George said, 'I've got a lot of fucking work to do with you lot so let's fucking get on with it,' and looking at Ray and Terry, added 'I'll see you two later.'

I took the two lads aside and said, 'Listen, you can't start like that. You get changed and we'll sort it out later.' That was the start of the George Petchey era and I was on my way to the States.

I had signed a two-year contract with Tampa Bay Rowdies and Gordon was scheduled to come back to the UK with the squad to train at Bisham Abbey in Buckinghamshire. I was to join them there and return with them to the US. By coincidence, I trained at Bisham Abbey with Tampa Bay and then returned later to the same location to train with the England team, of which more later.

On the first day at Bisham Abbey, Gordon introduced me to all the players. There were a couple I already knew, such as Rodney Marsh, and on that first day Gordon said to me, 'Why don't you take them out, have a little session with them and get to know them and I'll be out later.'

There were a few foreigners in there, Argentineans, Yugoslavs and the young Americans. So I did my normal routine, had a chat with the players and walked round with them before getting into a warm-up session.

After about five or ten minutes I saw Rodney Marsh and his little entourage of about six doing exactly the opposite of what I had said. The boys who were doing it properly were looking around thinking, 'What's going on here?' so I stopped the session and told them to gather round.

I walked straight up to Rodney and said to him 'Are you taking the piss?'

Rodney, in typical form, put his hands up in the air and said, 'No, why should I do that?'

'Because you're trying to make a point,' I said, 'and the point is you don't know me and maybe you don't rate me. But I'm telling you now, Rodney, that I've just signed a two-year contract at this place and, if you want to try to take me on, see those trees over there? You and I will go over there and we'll sort it out. Let me tell you now, I've never lost a fight in my life so if you fancy it just walk over there with me.'

There was deadly silence among the squad. I looked at Peter Anderson, a senior player who had played for Luton Town (a few years later I recommended him for the Millwall manager's job). I said, 'Peter, take charge while me and Rodney go over there.'

With that Rodney said, 'No, no, Ted, it's not a problem,' and backed off.

'Good,' I said. 'I'll tell you now, I've had to shoot people for less. So let's get down to work.'

I took that stand because I had been told previously that Rodney was the icon of the place and he liked his own way, so I realised I'd have to nip it in the bud. We never had a problem after that although for the next two years Rodney and Gordon never got on.

After Bisham the team flew to the US and a week later I flew over to Tampa. This was my first ever visit to the States and yet I was planning to live there for two years. I was expecting someone to meet me at Tampa Airport and as I came through customs there was Gordon, smiling all over his face, with two secretaries from the club. It was a nice surprise to see him there and the sort of thing that made him good at man management, making you feel that you're important and that you belong.

Tampa was paradise after wet and windy England. When they drove me to my apartment, everything was set up, washing machines, all the luxury goods that make life so much pleasanter and that I had never had in England. There were security guards on the electrified front gate and two burning torches outside that looked like the Olympic torch in front of the entrance – very impressive and a big change from South London.

When the season started in the North American Soccer League, we began quite well but the squad still needed strengthening. Our home stadium, which we shared with the Tampa Bay Buccaneers, the gridiron football team, held about 80 000 and we always got a crowd of between 40 000 and 50 000, which for a soccer team was excellent.

After each game, all the players, wives and girlfriends used to go to a restaurant. One night after a win, Gordon, George

Strawbridge, the owner of the club, and Chas Serednesky, the number two to Strawbridge, said that they thought we should get in some big names as there were a number of them in America at that time.

The New York Cosmos had all the Brazilians from the 1974 World Cup, Pelé being one of them. Franz Beckenbauer, the German captain, was also there but when Chas suggested that we bring them to the team, I said, 'Why should we do that? We shouldn't go for the big names like the Cosmos. There are people like Alan Ball, Peter Osgood (God bless them, they're both dead now), Harry Redknapp, Sam Allardyce and Tommy Smith from Liverpool. Let's go for the bread-and-butter players.'

George and Chas didn't know what I was talking about but Gordon understood. These were players who wanted to come out there not just for a holiday but to give 100 per cent when they were playing and would enjoy their time there. I said, 'They're the sort of players we need,' and to my surprise they agreed.

So we began to bring in the likes of Micky Maguire, Graham Paddon, Barry Kitchener from my old club Millwall and David Moss from Luton, starting a very successful couple of years with Tampa. They all did well for us and held their own with the big stars brought in from South America and Europe to the other clubs. Barry Kitchener stayed with us for just one season before his return to Millwall but he was so popular with the fans that more than 1000 people turned out to see him off at the airport on his departure.

We needed a full back so I went to watch three players. One was Allan Harris, Chopper's brother, at Chelsea; another, Dave Butler, was at Watford; another was John Gorman at Tottenham. I couldn't know it at the time, of course, but Allan Harris was later to become Terry Venables's assistant in Spain and would work with both me and Terry at Tottenham; Dave Butler finished up as England's physio with both England and Tottenham, working with Terry and me, and John Gorman was appointed Glenn Hoddle's assistant with England and followed the same path that I had trodden as Terry's assistant.

It was about this time that I became friends with Brian Moore, one of the best television commentators at the time. He came out and stayed with me with his wife Betty and sons, Chris and Simon. I took them all round Disneyworld and, when I finished that first season with Tampa and returned briefly to the UK, Brian invited me to his house in Orpington. At the time Brian thought that the American soccer side of things was about to take off and he was very impressed with what he had seen. We went to the Fantail Restaurant in Farnborough, Kent. I took Linda Doyle, the landlady from Forest Hill.

A few days before that meal that I had been down to Millwall and talked to George Petchey. Millwall was not having the best of times at that moment and I was in discussions with the hierarchy at Tampa about buying three of the best youngsters at Millwall who Gordon and I had brought into the club together with the help of Bob Pearson and Derek Healy. I made an offer for the three players, David Mehmet, Kevin O'Callaghan and Tony Kinsella.

Taking a bit of a chance, I asked George, 'How much do you want for the three lads?'

'I'll have to talk to the board, I have no idea,' he said.

'What if I put an idea into your head?' I asked. 'How about a million dollars?'

George nearly fell off his chair. 'Are you kidding?' he asked.

'No I'm not.'

'I'll have to speak to the board about this one,' he said. 'Can I let you know?'

I left it with him.

This was the backdrop to the conversation that I had with Brian at the Fantail Restaurant, which made headlines in the papers and put me on the map with the managers and chairmen of clubs in the UK, who now wanted to get in touch with me about certain players.

When I told Brian this story, he said 'Can I use it?'

'Certainly but wait until I get the clearance from Tampa and obviously only once Millwall accept,' I said.

But we met on Saturday night and by Monday morning it was headline news, which at the time was unheard of. I got a call from Tampa. I had already phoned Brian and said, 'I thought you were going to hold it' and he said he thought I had said it was OK.

Knowing Brian as I did, I knew he was not only an honest man but a terrific journalist so I wasn't too annoyed. In fact it put Tampa Bay Rowdies on the map and I think the hierarchy at Tampa was quite pleased with the outcome. As it turned out, it curtailed the system where players went out there on loan, because now the teams were looking for a fee for them. Perhaps I am in some way responsible for some of those changes in the game.

Eventually, we paid a price that was well short of a million because Kinsella and Mehmet were signed but Kevin O'Callaghan stayed at Millwall and was sold onto Ipswich Town. We also signed Nicky Johns, a young goalkeeper from Millwall. I suppose Kevin O'Callaghan's claim to fame was that he got a part in a Sylvester Stallone movie, *Escape To Victory*. While they were filming the movie, the Rowdies were invited to the premier but prior to it I had met a young co-producer on the film, who was responsible for the invitation.

I took her out to lunch one day and she told me about the film: Michael Caine was the main star. Bobby Moore, Ossie Ardiles and Pelé were also in it. Kevin O'Callaghan was the original goalkeeper in the film – he was only five foot eight which was a bit short for a keeper, so in my opinion he was a bit miscast. The story was that Michael Caine and Bobby Moore told young Kevin that his arm had to be deliberately broken in the film to make way for

Sylvester Stallone's character to take over as goalkeeper. In the film Kevin didn't flinch when they broke his arm which was so unrealistic – I couldn't believe they could get away with that – but that's Hollywood.

When the co-producer was telling me about the script, she suddenly turned round to me and said, 'Michael is not a great footballer and we have problems when we get shots of him with the ball.' She added that I talked like him.

I said I come from the same part of the country as him, South London; him from the Elephant and Castle and me from Deptford. 'Not a lot of people know that,' I added.

She didn't smile and clearly didn't get the joke. 'Perhaps if I could get you down to the set, we could film your legs and, as you sound like him when you speak, we could use your legs and voice without showing your face,' she said.

In the event, I couldn't get an Equity card, so my legs never graced the silver screen and my Hollywood career died before it started.

After the 1978 World Cup, Chas Serednesky and Gordon Jago got a call from a Polish agent, who was well connected in America. He let them know that two Polish players, the captain of the Polish national team, Grzegorz Lato, and Andrzej Szarmach, both strikers who played for Stal Mielec in the Polish league, would be available for a loan to Tampa Bay Rowdies. As Chas and Gordon pointed out, with Poland being behind the Iron Curtain at the time, it might be a bit tricky to persuade the authorities to allow them to come out of the country. After a lengthy discussion among the three of us as to who should go to Poland to meet up with the agent and players, Gordon and Chas asked me if I fancied going. I was up for a challenge so I agreed.

I flew into Warsaw and was met by the agent. My first impression of the country was that it was the dullest and most depressing place I had seen for a long time. Apart from the fact that it was drizzling with rain and the people walking around looked utterly miserable as we drove to the hotel in Warsaw, there was a big monument in the middle of a square with an enormous hammer and sickle on top, which did nothing to lighten the mood.

After checking into the hotel, I was met in the foyer by the agent, accompanied by two heavies. They ushered me outside into a waiting car with blacked-out windows. The agent got in the front and I was put in the back between the heavies. It all seemed a bit cloak and dagger, like something out of a spy novel. Only the agent spoke, saying we wouldn't take long to get to our destination but we must be careful.

Now I was getting suspicious. 'What's the problem then?' I asked.

'Certain persons would be unhappy at losing two special players,' he replied. From then on I kept quiet. Eventually we pulled into a small hotel just outside Warsaw. There was a small alley running along the back. The car drove down it and stopped outside a side entrance. The agent got out and the door opened. I was quickly ushered down a flight of stairs into a small concrete room with only one small window high up. The two heavies followed. As they closed the door they stood alongside it looking straight ahead, utterly silent and emotionless.

There, in the middle of the room sitting at a square table, were the two players, Lato and Szarmach. Both stood and half-bowed before shaking hands with me. 'Pleased to meet you,' said Lato in his broken English.

With that there was a knock on the door and another guy was ushered in. He sat straight down, held out his hand to me and just said 'Mr Buxton' before switching into Polish to the players and the agent. At intervals they explained in English the terms they wanted. I agreed a $300 000 fee for the loan of the two players for the American season, which lasted from the end of their season in April until September. I also insisted on guarantees that they would be able to finish the loan period without being recalled and we then signed the agreements between us.

We shook hands all round and the two players looked pleased but a bit overwhelmed. I was simply happy that we had two quality players, so I went back to the hotel in the same way, under heavy secrecy. When they dropped me back, they swiftly disappeared into the night, with the agent telling me in the car that he would see me on my departure at the airport on the following afternoon.

I had a meal alone in the hotel with a couple of glasses of questionable Polish wine and then had a brief stroll outside. Apparently there had been a local football match somewhere and the crowd of spectators coming from the game looked drunk and very volatile so I went back to the hotel, well satisfied with the success of the day.

The following morning I had breakfast and decided to go out and have a look around Warsaw on my own. It was a most depressing experience. There were long queues outside all the food shops and stalls and as I walked past I could see that there was hardly any actual food in the shops. The people were dressed in drab grey clothing and there was no colour anywhere. The overcast weather did nothing for the sombre mood and I was struck by the huge contrast between their lives and the lifestyle I had been enjoying in America.

As I was wandering back to the hotel, a taxi drew alongside me and the driver in English asked if he could help me. I told him I was fine and he then said, 'Can I have a word with you? You're from England? Are you going home to England?'

I told him I was going home to America later that day. He said he could come and pick me up, which I said was fine and he then said, 'You would do me a great honour. I have a fur coat you could wear under your big coat and walk through customs.'

I asked why I would do that and he said I could make money and so could he. 'And I need the money,' he continued. I wasn't about to break any rules in that place and told him to forget about picking me up. I would find my own way to the airport. But that wasn't the end of it because as I walked into the hotel and got my room key, one of the hotel staff followed me into the lift and asked me if I was going back to America and if I would like to buy some Levi jeans very cheap.

I declined and started to realise that everyone in the country was so desperate that they wouldn't miss an opportunity to try to make some money to improve their situation, regardless of the risks they might have to take in doing so. I was not unhappy to leave this sad place behind but could at least regard the trip as a success because of the deal that had been signed.

When I got back to America, Gordon and the owners were pleased with the outcome and we were looking forward to the season coming up with the new players on board. However, only a few weeks later it all fell apart. Tampa got a call from someone at the Polish FA to say that the two players, along with others, had been disciplined for some misdemeanour and suspended by their clubs and consequently would not be allowed to leave the country.

I was bitterly disappointed that the players didn't have the chance to come and show their qualities with the Rowdies because I am sure they would have been a great success. I can understand now after what I had seen of Poland that the country was ripe for change and I was not surprised some years later when Lech Wałęsa became prominent in Polish politics, paving the way for the new modern Poland and leaving the Communist era behind.

ADVENTURES IN THE BEAUTIFUL GAME

After that first year in Tampa, we had got to our first NASL (North American Soccer League) final against the New York Cosmos. We flew into New York and stayed at the Plaza Hotel beside Central Park. Two players had injuries: Rodney Marsh had a problem with a leg strain and Micky Maguire had a horrendous Achilles tendon problem – he was recovering after an operation and his calf was sore but he was determined to play in the final. Rodney too said he would play but he would give it one more go at a try-out in Central Park.

I took both of them out in the morning and put them through a little light session. We got back to the hotel where Gordon met us and asked how it went. 'No problem – the old British Bulldog, heart as big as a cabbage,' said Rodney.

Gordon accordingly selected both of them to play. After our pre-match meal the players were going off to rest before we went to the game when Rodney informed us that he wasn't fit enough to play after all. I personally felt that Rodney didn't want to be second best and he feared he would be outdone by the Cosmos and the stars that were playing for them. Talk about a heart as big as a cabbage! Micky Maguire, on the other hand, got through an hour of the game, worked his socks off and could hardly walk when we eventually took him off after an hour but the team had done well against all the stars that were on show for the Cosmos.

Even so, we lost 3–1. Who knows how we would have done if Rodney had played? Rodney could have matched the Cosmos players for ability and technique and maybe if he had played that day he could have turned the game in our favour. But that's history now.

In Rodney's last game as a Rowdy in the League, Gordon decided to substitute one of the young Americans for Rodney, much to the surprise not only of me but also, most of the subs on the bench. Gordon turned to me and said, 'Tell Rodney he's got two minutes.'

Rodney came over and I said, 'Rodney you've got two minutes.'

He stood and glared at Gordon. The ball came to him and then we saw the best of Rodney Marsh: he went past three players, who never got near him, with tremendous close control. He hit the shot from twenty-five yards, smashed against the post and went out for a goal kick. He never hesitated. He turned around, took his shirt off and walked straight off the pitch, slinging his shirt between me and Gordon and went straight into the locker room, as we called it, not the dressing room. That was Rodney's last game for Tampa Bay Rowdies until his testimonial.

Rodney had been signed by the previous management at Tampa and he and Gordon had never really got on. Nevertheless, they promised him a testimonial, which was unheard of in America. In the end when it came around we played an all-star team that had crossed America to take part. He had a great turnout, a crowd of 35000 to 40000 were in the stadium to watch the game. Gordon refused to coach it because of the atmosphere between the two of them so Rodney asked me to do it because it was a big-sell out in the Rowdies stadium.

I spoke to Gordon and the powers that be and they decided that I'd take the team to save any aggravation. I think that Rodney appreciated that, although we were never best mates. Years later when I was with Tottenham, he apparently was out with Terry

Venables one night and Terry asked Rodney how he got on with me. 'I thought we did OK but Ted was a bit slippery. You never knew where he was coming from,' Terry told me he'd said.

When I met up with Rodney some time later I mentioned this to him and he said, 'No, I didn't say slippery. I just said I didn't know where you were coming from.' That was Rodney, often backtracking, so I don't really know what he thought but I know I have been mentioned a few times by him on Talk Sport.

During a visit to Tampa, Brian Moore, who was a good friend of Brian Clough, came out to stay with me. He was about to commentate on the forthcoming European Cup Final between Nottingham Forest and Malmo. I had just been to Malmo to see a player and Brian asked me if I remembered the shape of the team and its set plays. When I confirmed that I always make notes after the games I watch and could remember the team well, he surprised me by asking if I would do a report for Nottingham Forest. I gave him a brief written report, which he gave to Peter Taylor, assistant manager to Brian Clough. After Nottingham Forest won the European Cup 1–0 with Trevor Francis, their record signing from Birmingham, scoring the winning goal, Brian told me that Cloughie had sent Jimmy Gordon with my report to Malmo to see them play before the final. Nottingham Forest subsequently came out to Tampa to play an exhibition game.

At the end of the season I flew to Buenos Aires to look at a player at the River Plate football stadium, flying down the river itself and experiencing beautiful views. The stadium nestling beside the river was magnificent from the sky, all in red and white. The player wasn't available so I flew on to Uruguay and Chile. In Chile I wanted to sign a boy, a winger, but they wanted too much money for him. I had already sussed out a boy in the Club Atlético Peñarol club in Uruguay and also saw a boy called Washington Olivera. He was a Uruguayan international playing in the same position as Rodney, a left-sided player, all left foot, great technical ability and with a charismatic personality. After long negotiations we managed to sign him for $150 000.

During my time with Tampa, I invited my ex-wife Joyce to come over to spend a couple of weeks' holiday in America. Although we had divorced in 1978, we remained on good terms and are still friends today. As I was away travelling, Nancy, one of the secretaries, looked after Joyce as she did with my sons, Vince and John, when they came out to visit. I was a little worried at that time that Joyce was hoping for a reconciliation although I don't think I gave her that impression.

I bought her a gold Indian arrow head as a necklace. She was delighted until Chas Serednesky invited all the staff round to his house for a barbecue party around his pool. He invited Joyce too as it was one of her last nights in Tampa, so I picked her up from the hotel where she was staying. She was wearing the necklace I had bought. Unfortunately, as we walked into the pool area in Chas's garden, Nancy came in, wearing the same necklace that I had bought for her some months previously. The two of them looked at each other and it was like the stand-off at the O.K. Corral. So the evening didn't go too well. My mistake was to buy two women the same gift – lesson learned.

We had had a tip off from Petrovic, an ex-player with Red Star Belgrade, that a boy called Petar Baralić, a Yugoslav under-21 international, was available. I flew to Belgrade to see him play in an under-21 game and decided that he would be really good for us – a good mid-fielder, a box-to-box player, who had strength and good technical ability. It was decided to try to get him to the club but the problem was he had to be a full International to get a work permit and a player's visa. Petrovic, the agent, said it wouldn't be a problem so the powers to be (namely Gordon Jago and Chas Serednesky) arranged the fee and I was to fly back to Belgrade to see him play a full international game while I was there.

Petrovic met me at the airport and we went to the hotel where he said that we would be going to a nightclub that night to relax. When we got into the club it was not what I expected because the opening show was topless girls, which I didn't think was the sort of entertainment a Communist country would allow. I settled down to enjoy myself. The music had died down and there was a bit of a lull in proceedings when Petrovic said, 'There's just one little problem. The club needs another $10 000 on the fee to meet expenses and to make sure that the boy gets his cap.'

With that he said that he had arranged it with Miljan Miljanić, who was the Yugoslav national coach, who later on was offered the job of Chelsea manager. Once I had been told this and knowing we wanted to get the boy, I had to agree not knowing quite what the extra expenses were. But I thought at the time that with the fee we were paying for him, which was about $150 000, this was still a good bet. So I agreed.

We got through another bottle of wine and a singer had come on and sung a couple of songs and the dancing girls had come on again when all of a sudden the music stopped dead. Everything went quiet and people started standing up. I looked over to the stairway and a figure was standing on the top of the stairs, immaculately dressed with a light blue overcoat draped around his shoulders. On his arm was a beautiful blonde woman. Now everybody was on their feet clapping. At the time I really thought it was General Tito, the Yugoslav President.

Petrovic leaned across and whispered in my ear, 'It's Miljanić.'

He walked down the stairs with his lady and made his way straight to our table where he said, 'Mr Buxton, pleased to meet you. Has Petrovic mentioned the arrangements?'

'Yes, that's fine, no problems,' I said.

'Tomorrow we go to the game together,' he replied. 'We will fly to Titograd and the boy will definitely play. I'll see you at the airport in the morning. Have a good evening.' He spoke perfect English.

In the morning I got to the airport with Petrovic. The plane was ready to leave but nobody was moving until Miljanić showed up. He arrived, said, 'You sit with me,' and no one moved to get onto the plane until we had got on.

We flew into Titograd (now commonly known as Podgorica), had refreshments with Petrovic and a few dignitaries and watched the game. Some of the dignitaries were army people. I didn't get the significance of that until a few days later. We watched the game and the boy played well. We got back to the hotel in Titograd and Petrovic said, 'We're going out for the night.'

It was the same scenario. Nightclub, dancing girls, singers, when all of a sudden the band stopped playing and everybody stood up again. Again the clapping started. Another grand entrance by Miljanić but this time on his arm was an older lady with glasses who looked like the girl Olive from *On The Buses*. He came straight to us at the table. I stood up and shook his hand. He said, 'Mr Buxton, this is my wife. Did you enjoy the game?'

'Very much,' I replied.

'Everything's done,' he said. 'The boy can come to America.'

'Thank you very much. Mum's the word,' I replied, in reference to the lovely lady that had accompanied him in Belgrade.

I don't know if he understood but he did say, 'Thank you very much – pleasure to meet you.'

After the game we flew back to Belgrade when Petrovic said we were going to have lunch at the hotel. 'I want you to meet a couple of military men who are involved in Red Star Belgrade, for whom the boy Petar Baralić plays,' he said.

As we sat down for a meal the two military men came in and one of them turned out to be Radovan Karadžić, later implicated for war crimes. The younger one was Ratko Mladic, the man many hold responsible for the worst atrocities in the Bosnian war. On the day itself, we had a nice meal and a friendly chat and I had no notion then of the different factions in Yugoslavia that caused all the problems later.

Karadžić was telling me about the factions and the problems they had with the Muslims. Tito was ill at the time and Karadžić was telling me that if Tito died the Muslims would try to take over Yugoslavia.

'If that happened, I would mobilise 30 000 Serbs and we would destroy them,' he said forcefully. At the time it didn't mean too much to me but now I know that a few years later that really happened in Yugoslavia and terrible atrocities were committed.

At the time I thought, 'Christ, this is a real patriot. I'd like him on my side in a war.' It just goes to show that you can't always take things at face value.

We shook hands and I went back to my room, ready to leave in the morning to fly back to the UK where I was due to meet Lawrie McMenemy about a full back called Manny Andruszewski, a good player who was coming out on loan. We eventually bought him outright. Manny was a hell of a full back and did very well. Unfortunately, in later years he started suffering from illness and had to pack up but I've seen him from time to time and he's fine, making a new career in landscape gardening.

Lawrie used to come out to Tampa on visits with his wife, Anne, and his boys and liked the place so much that he eventually bought a place.

I next flew out to Honduras via Belize to watch a recommended player. When I got on the plane in Belize it was a nightmare. They were loading up crates of live chickens, piglets and a few other animals including goats, which were all stored in the passenger cabin of the plane. I had been previously told that the landing was a bit scary and I didn't realise how scary. You flew through mountains that looked so close they seemed to be touching the wings of the plane and then suddenly you're coming down on an airstrip that overlooks the sea. The runway must have been just about a 1000 yards. We hit the runway and I felt we were going too fast – we finished up about 100 yards from the end of the runway with sea in front of us. I said to some guy on the plane, 'Christ, that was a bit close'.

'That's usual,' he said. 'They've got it timed to a second.'

I thought, 'Well, I suppose they do this every day'.

I then got a taxi into Tegucigalpa, the capital of Honduras. In those days, the seventies, there was just an airport, a church and a hotel. When the taxi driver picked me up, I found he spoke English and he said, 'We have to pick up someone else on the way.'

I had already put my bags, emblazoned with Tampa Bay Rowdies all over them, in the back of his boot. When we went through a little village to pick up this guy the driver said, 'We must just drop him up the road'.

Having picked him up, we went a short distance before arriving at a café-type place. He didn't have any bags with him so he and the driver got out of the car and, when I looked out of the car, the guy had got two of my bags on his shoulder and he was walking off with them. I got out of the car, grabbed him by the collar and said 'Oi!'

He obviously didn't speak English but the driver explained, 'I am very sorry. He thought that this was where you were going to stop to eat.' I thought I'd heard some stories in my time but that topped the lot so I wasn't too happy right from the outset.

The game I had come to see was Honduras versus El Salvador, and it was just such a game that in the past had started a war between the two countries. It had only recently been resolved so this game was a one-off. I couldn't believe the poverty at the time – beggars on the street, disabled people crawling around, kids asking for money – it was unbelievable. The beaches and the sea were absolute paradise and I thought it was such a waste. As far as the game went, it was very physical and I came to the conclusion that the player I had come to see, a striker, was no better than the players we had back in Tampa.

I flew out of Honduras back to Belize to get a plane back to Miami and was sitting by the window in first class when a guy sat next to me. He was grey-haired and tanned. At first I thought it was Cesar Romero, the film star. I remember he had a light blue jacket on and looked very distinguished. I didn't like to ask him if he was Cesar Romero but when he looked at one of my bags and saw Tampa Bay Rowdies on it he said, 'Are you into soccer?'

We began to chat and after a couple of bottles of wine, he started to open up. He asked me about the Rowdies and about England and said he had been to London and enjoyed it. I eventually said to him, 'And what do you do?'

'I'm a lawyer for Metro Goldwyn Mayer, the film people,' he replied. He said he had just got back from Nicaragua and he started telling me a story that was unbelievable.

A couple of years or so previously, the company had been making a film in Nicaragua starring Anthony Quinn and, during one of the breaks they had in filming, a few of the crew went on a bit of a bender, got pissed (as he said) and coming back in the Jeep, came off the side of the road and smashed into a shanty village, killing a couple of locals. When it all came out, he said, Louis B Mayer of MGM flew him out there to negotiate with the then president who was part of the military junta.

Mayer told him to pay out whatever it took to resolve it, even if it took a million dollars for each person. This had been agreed with one of the generals of the junta and the money had been paid. The lawyer had to fly to Nicaragua to catch the plane to Belize but he said that when he got to Nicaragua, before he could board, he was told that the plane was going to be held up and he must come and meet the same general who had received the payment.

The general took him to his ranch and the lawyer said he tried to explain that he had to get back for the plane. The general said that wasn't a problem as the plane would wait for him, but he had to see what had been achieved with MGM's money. The ranch was palatial and he said as they walked around, the general said, 'I must extend. I need to bring in thoroughbred horses and you might be able to help us if you could come back, make another film and kill a few more peasants.'

I asked the lawyer if the story was true and he said 'Absolutely'.

I could hardly believe that these sorts of things went on. We said our goodbyes in Miami as I had to catch a plane into Tampa. He said, 'If you're ever in LA, look me up,' but that was it. I don't know if he was so well-known that he thought I would know who he was but he didn't give me a card so I couldn't have looked him up. It certainly wasn't Cesar Romero.

SAVAGERY IN THE DESERT

I was doing a lot of travelling for Tampa, looking at players in Europe and South America, and had just got back from a trip to Honduras when, in spring 1980, I received a call from my sister, Edie, to tell me that my mum was seriously ill in a hospice in Sydenham and that I needed to get home to see her. The club arranged everything immediately; flights home and whatever time I needed, so I flew back to Heathrow and was met by my sons, Vince and John.

I stayed for a couple of days at the hospice with my mum. She was drifting in and out of consciousness but I think she knew I was there. Every time I spoke to her she squeezed my hand. Then she seemed to rally a bit and one of the doctors said that she seemed to be holding her own. When I asked how long it might be, he told me it could go on like that for weeks. I stayed with her and the family for the whole week, keeping in touch with the club by phone as there were some important games coming up.

After consulting with the doctors I decided to fly back to America on the Monday morning. Again everything was arranged by the club. On the Sunday I sat with mum all day and she seemed to respond and then I told her that I would have to go back but I had arranged that the hospice would have a phone by her bed so that I could phone her every day. With that she squeezed my hand. I kissed her and said my goodbyes. 'I'll speak to you as soon as I get back,' I said.

I flew into Tampa and was met by one of the secretaries, Nancy, to say that my ex-wife Joyce, had phoned to say that my mother was in her last hours and that the club had arranged tickets and transport to fly me straight back to the UK. Within a few hours I had turned tail and was on my way back to the UK but, while I was in the air, mum died peacefully.

My sister said to me, 'I think that once she had seen you, she gave up and was ready to go.'

I phoned the club and said I would come back as soon as the funeral was over. On the day of the funeral, three enormous baskets of flowers were delivered to the church: one from the players, one from the owner and one from the staff. I was overwhelmed by their generosity and warmth. They do everything in a big way in America and with a big heart. I shall always have fond memories of the club and the people in it.

When I got back to the States, I threw myself straight back into training and the club games. We had a tip about a centre forward, Thomas Sjöberg. He was formerly with Malmo and was now playing for Etihad in Jeddah. The problem was that the Chicago White Caps had also negotiated with him to go and play in America but apparently they hadn't followed up so I flew out to the Middle East and booked myself into the Marriott Hotel in Jeddah. My room had a small balcony overlooking a vast space with a mosque at one end of it. When I looked out the first time there were kids playing in the square and everything was normal.

I then had to set out to find Thomas Sjöberg and it was two days before I discovered that he was being put up by a Swedish company way out in the desert. A taxi driver befriended me in the course of those two days and I found out from someone in the Swedish Embassy where to get to this Swedish complex. My Arab driver said he knew where it was so off we went the next morning and it seemed as if we were driving for ages through the desert. Just when I thought I might be being kidnapped, from out of the sand dunes came this fort-like structure – it looked like something out of the Old West.

We stopped outside two great wooden doors with a huge Saudi standing guard outside – he must have been about six foot six tall, with what looked like an old fashioned rifle. As he came over to us I said, 'I am here to see Thomas Sjöberg.'

Fortunately he understood a little bit of English and he came out with the word 'football'.

'Yes, that's him,' I said. With that he bellowed something and the one door opened.

'You go,' he said.

My cab driver was trying to follow me in when the guard grabbed hold of him and virtually slung him a couple of yards in the air. He said something in Arabic and the fellow rushed back to sit in his cab.

I put my hand up and said, 'Wait.'

'OK,' he said.

With that, someone inside the complex came over to me and in near perfect English (he was a Swede) said, 'You want to see Thomas Sjöberg?'

'Yes, that's right,' I said.

'He is not here but you can talk to his wife,' he replied. Then he showed me round the edge of a big swimming pool and sitting with a young girl of about eight was a very attractive, blond lady. She was in a bikini but she had a big burn scar down one arm.

She spoke good English and said, 'We've been expecting you.' She ordered me a drink, not alcohol, because it was apparently not allowed, although being a Swedish complex I believe they could bend the rules. We sat down and talked and she said, 'I'm sorry but Thomas is training and he won't be back for a few hours.'

'It's not a problem, now that I know where the place is,' I said. 'I'll come back tonight and talk.'

Then she said something that took me aback. 'No, you mustn't come out here at night. We will come to your hotel.'

'It's not a problem for me to come,' I said.

'No you mustn't come here. It could be dangerous,' she replied. She promised that she and Thomas would see me in the hotel that evening.

They turned up on time and I took them to the restaurant where we had a drink – soft drinks again – and a meal and started to talk. Thomas said that Chicago had negotiated with his club, Malmo, but he hadn't heard anything and he needed to get out of Jeddah as soon as possible.

I asked what sort of money he wanted and we talked about life in Tampa and what a good place it was to bring up children. I had a blank contract with me and said, 'Do you want to go through the contract and negotiate the money?'

'I will sign it now,' he said.

When I said we should fill in the details he simply said, 'I will trust you and when we get to Florida we can fill in the details.'

I was quite surprised by that because I had never had any experience before of anyone signing a blank contract but I got the impression that he needed to get out of the place as quickly as possible. Back at the hotel, I got in touch with the powers that be in Tampa and they were absolutely delighted. I had another two days in Jeddah seeing the sights and was due to fly back on the Saturday.

On Thursday evening I had an early meal followed by an early night. I was exhausted after all the running around. Early on Friday morning I was awakened by what sounded like guns going off. I got up and looked over the square where normally all the kids would be playing and saw a crowd of people and a guy dressed in white being dragged to what looked like a stone monument in the middle of the square. He was forced down on his knees and a guy in a uniform with a big sabre promptly went to his side and lopped off his head. I have seen some sights, certainly in Malaya in my army days, but never anything like that.

I pulled away and got off the balcony as quickly as I could and got dressed. Outside the hotel was my cab driver waiting for me. I said, 'What's going on?'

'Execution day,' he replied in his broken English.

I asked a white guy who I think was Swedish and probably from the Embassy for more information. He told me that they had just executed that man for adultery. He had allegedly been having an affair with the wife of a Saudi army man. I didn't know whether to believe him when he said that she should have been stoned to death, but because of her status they had shot her.

That night when I went back up to my room there was one hell of a storm. Hailstones as big as marbles were raining down, flooding the square and all the roads outside – there seemed to be no drainage at all – and I wondered if this downpour was an act of God because they hadn't experienced a storm like it in years. I was glad to get back on that plane and back to Tampa. I've never been to Jeddah since and have never wanted to go back.

Back in Tampa, we had a break before Thanksgiving, when I got a call from Ron Newman, the coach of Fort Lauderdale. He said, 'I know you've got a ten-day break. Any chance of bringing a team down to play us?' He added that George Best had been away for about six weeks and had just got back and that he needed to get him playing again.

So I said to Gordon Jago, 'How about it?' and he got the OK from the Chief Exec. The only problem was that we had to fly down there, which was a 400-mile trip, and play in the afternoon, in temperatures of about 95 degrees. So Gordon said to take all the fringe players and the young Americans.

We flew into Fort Lauderdale, booked into a hotel near 66 Pier and got to the ground where it was stiflingly hot and very humid. Ron Newman came over and had a chat with us and the players and said that he was only going to play the kids, by which he meant the young Americans and, of course, George Best. I had a chat with George and asked how he was. He looked as fit as a flea. 'How are your women problems, George?' I asked.

'No problems. Come and have a drink afterwards before you fly back,' he said.

We went into the dressing room and got changed. They had arranged a referee so we gave our team sheets to the referee and I went back and started my team talk. I wrote the Fort Lauderdale team up on the white board and looking at their team sheet it seemed as if George was playing wide on the left, left midfield as it is now called. We had a young American playing at right back, who was obviously going to mark George. When he came over to me he asked, 'How do I play him?'

'Listen,' I said. 'George has been on the piss for a couple of months and he's not trained. It's 95 degrees out there and stifling. Just keep him wide on the left. Don't let him come inside and if he does come inside, pass him on, meaning the centre back or the midfield players will pick him up. It's easier for you to keep him wide.'

So the game started and at half time we were 3–0 down and George had scored two goals. He had run us ragged. Outside and inside he was outstanding. After an hour, Ron Newman took him off, to give us a bit of a respite and the game finished up 4–2 to them. So much for my advice, but that was George. On a good day he was unbeatable. I went and had a drink with him in his hotel and all he had was lager. I had my usual glass of wine and we sat there chatting about different things for a while when two or three attractive, young girls came round the pool and started chatting to George. He said, 'I'm busy at the moment, girls. Maybe I'll see you later.'

With that, they went off. 'Is this what you get all the time, George?' I asked.

'Yes, just a little,' he replied, adding, 'Life's a bitch.'

Years later, when George had his liver problems, I went down to Portsmouth to watch a player. The chairman, Milan Mandarić, asked me to come down to the boardroom at half time to see George, who was undergoing treatment. He was just drinking tonic water, though whether there was anything in it I would not have known but he looked OK, if a bit drawn.

We talked about old times and America and that was the last time I spoke to him. What a waste of a talent and, to me, a top man and a gentleman. I can understand how his charisma drew women to him. He didn't even have to try. I had been at a function when he was with Mary Stävin, an ex-Miss World, and that night I could see how much she loved him.

Soon afterwards we received information that Peter Nogly, the captain of Hamburg SV, was available for a free transfer so I flew out to Germany to meet him and his wife to see whether he would be interested in coming to America. The two of them came to meet me at the hotel and at the time there was a beer festival going on. It was about the same time that the agent acting for Felix Magath and Ivan Buljan, both internationals, said they could also be available to come to America, if the deal was right. First, Peter Nogly agreed in principle to negotiate with the hierarchy in Tampa to come at the end of that season. In the meantime, Dennis Roach, the agent negotiating for both Buljan and Magath, the German national captain, said the fee would be $300 000.

Boosted by this information I spoke with Gordon and Chas and Gordon decided to fly out and seal the deal. Before he did so I met Dennis Roach for dinner, during which he said to me, 'There'll be a nice bit of commission for you and Gordon.'

'What are you on about?' I asked.

'Well, there'll be $40 000 in there for you and Gordon as a finder's bonus,' he said.

I had never before been offered that kind of money or anything like it. When Gordon flew in he was quite excited about the players.

We were still waiting for a decision from Peter Nogly but that was on hold. Gordon and I went out for a meal together the night he flew in and I then told him about the offer by Roach. Gordon said, 'What's he talking about $40 000?'

'That's apparently the commission you get,' I replied.

'Tell him to knock it off the $300 000 fee,' said Gordon. When I told Dennis Roach he said it couldn't be done because it was separate from the fee. With that, Gordon said the deal was off. In the meantime I stayed on to try to seal the other deal with Peter Nogly but after a few more days he had decided that he didn't want to go to America. So it was disappointing that we lost out on three good players.

I stayed for a couple more days before getting a flight out of Hamburg back to Miami. In the VIP departure lounge, I was having a glass of wine when in walked Ella Fitzgerald, surrounded by her entourage. She looked in my direction, spotted my bags bearing the Tampa Bay Rowdies emblem and said, 'Are you into soccer?'

I confirmed that I was with the Rowdies and she said, 'I'm a big supporter of Leeds United Football Club. I performed there some years ago and still look for their results.'

I was quite impressed with that and then she asked me about myself and we had a nice chat. As we walked up to the plane (we were all travelling first class) she insisted that I sat with her, making her companion who I think was her agent or her husband, sit elsewhere. She was an amazing woman and a great conversationalist.

As we left the plane in Miami, from where she was flying off to Los Angeles, she asked one of her lady companions to get a photo, signed it for me and promptly said, 'If you're anywhere around and I'm performing, don't hesitate to ask to see the show and maybe we can have a meal afterwards.' It's a photo I've still got and will always cherish. Unfortunately, I never got to take up her invitation.

I was coming towards the end of my contract with Tampa and they asked me if I wanted to stay on for another year but I had a feeling that Gordon's relationship with the Tampa Bay fans was waning. I don't think that Gordon was happy and he was looking to move elsewhere. I got a call from Keith Peacock, who was now the manager at Gillingham, where he had taken over from Gerry Summers. I had recommended Keith for the job when Brian Moore and his family had stayed with me in Tampa and Brian had asked if I fancied going back and having a job at Gillingham. At that time I had still had a year to go on my contract so I had recommended Keith.

So Keith, who knew that my contract was coming to an end, asked me if I fancied joining him at Gillingham as assistant and chief scout. He already had a lad called Paul Taylor as coach, who he had brought in from America. I decided that after three great years at Tampa it was time to move on and go back home so at the end of the American season I said my farewells. But I had an open invitation from the chief exec and the owner, George Strawbridge, to go back whenever I wanted. They would arrange it as a working holiday, coaching in the local community.

BACK TO BLIGHTY – PART ONE

I flew back at the start of the UK pre-season, around June or July 1982, and returned to my flat in Nunhead in Peckham, which I had left in the care of my neighbours. Either side of me I had nice elderly couples who had looked after the garden for me. My sister, Edie, used to go down and clean the place and my brother-in-law looked after the maintenance to ensure everything was working properly and maintained my car, an old Cortina. Unfortunately, by the time I got back, my poor old neighbours on both sides had died and immigrants had moved in to both flats either side. I had a stand-off with one set of new neighbours within a week.

I came home from training one night with Gillingham. I went out to have a meal in my favourite steak house in Camberwell, went home and went to bed. At about two o'clock in the morning I was woken by the loud rhythmic thumping of reggae music next door. After about fifteen minutes, I got up and got dressed. I went next door and banged loudly on the door. A Jamaican man and his wife came down and he asked, 'What's your problem, man?'

Red mist descended. 'You're the fucking problem,' I said. 'Cut the music out as I've got to go to work in the morning – I can't laze around all day on benefits.' With that I put my hand under my jacket and said, 'Turn it down or you'll have a problem.'

They clearly assumed I had a weapon and his wife said, 'No problems.'

▲ On patrol

▼ Platoon celebration

With Washington Olivera in the Tampa stadium

Still in Tampa, with Nicky Johns and Rodney Marsh

With Jimmy Gordon and Peter Taylor

In Tampa with Wes McLeod

My sons,
Vince and John ▶

Together with
Mum and Alfie ▼

▲ With George Best

▼ Gillingham team photo

▲ A signed photo of Ella Fitzgerald

Me and Gary Lineker, after signing from Barcelona ▲

▼ Getting the Tottenham job!
◀ Me with Paul Stewart
↘ At Tottenham vets team charity match

With Glenn Hoddle ▼

▲ Chris Waddle, signed to Tottenham

▼ With Gazza

'There had better not be or I'll be back,' I said. By the time I got back into my flat, the music had been turned off.

About a week later, I had come home after training when there was a knock at my door. Standing on the doorstep was the same guy, who said 'Everything alright?'

'Yes, everything is fine,' I replied.

He said, 'We'd like to apologise for last week but we just had a new baby boy and he's being baptised soon. We'd like you to be his godfather.'

'You must be kidding!'

'We'd love you to,' he said. 'Would you like to come up and see the baby?'

So, being a good neighbour, I went up there. They asked if I'd like a drink, a beer or something so I had my usual glass of wine. There must have been ten of them up there, all relatives and friends. Then his wife walked out of the bedroom with the baby and said, 'There he is and we would love you to be his godfather.'

They were all very pleasant and even asked me to hold the baby. I looked around and said, 'Listen, you must have many friends and relatives who would love to be the godfather and I'm honoured that you even asked me but I don't think I'm the godfather type.' With that I wished them good night. To be fair, they were always very friendly and I never had any problems after that. I wonder if they were thinking of Marlon Brando, the godfather from the movie, when they asked me to be the godfather?

In my first season at Gillingham, Keith Peacock's brother-in-law, Peter, who worked as physio for another club in the Kent league, came in to see Keith and during a conversation I asked him how he had got on the previous Saturday. He told me that they had played Crockenhill. They were badly beaten and it was down to Crockenhill's striker, a lad called Tony Cascarino. After Peter left, I had a word with Keith because we had already agreed that we needed another striker and I arranged to go and see this player.

He was powerful in the air, had a great left foot and, although averagely paced, he had good technical ability on the floor so I decided on the strength of that one game that he would be good enough to bring in to Gillingham. That night I had a word with the Crockenhill manager/secretary and asked him if I could take Cascarino to Gillingham to train with us for a week to see how he performed with the pros.

He said they had a league game that week followed by a game where Cascarino was to represent the league so it would be difficult for him to come to Gillingham. So I sent Bob Dennison, ex-Coventry manager, who was also the father of Gillingham's secretary, Richard, to go to watch Cascarino at this next game. He came back with similarly glowing reports so I then sat down with Keith and agreed that I would go back to watch the lad in the representative game and would then meet with the manager.

When I arrived at the game I met the Crockenhill manager, who invited me to sit with him in the directors' box. On the other side of the pitch I could see a number of scouts from league clubs who were obviously there to watch Cascarino. One was Bob Pearson, who I had previously worked with at Millwall and who later went on to manage the club. Cascarino had a quiet game and didn't do anything to impress the onlookers so twenty minutes before the end, I watched all of the other scouts leaving the game, clearly not particularly impressed. Being in the directors' box with the manager, I of course stayed on. It was then that Cascarino came into his own. He scored two great goals to win the game so I had a serious chat with the manager. He agreed to my proposal for Cascarino to come to Gillingham to train with us.

I asked Tony if he had ever trained with a pro club and he confirmed that he had done with Queens Park Rangers, but it hadn't worked out. He mentioned that it had been a long way to travel and he had been late a few times because of traffic. I rang Theo Foley, who had worked with me and Gordon Jago at Millwall and was now at QPR, to get the background information on Cascarino. He told me I was wasting my time because we wouldn't get him out of bed. I felt some misgivings but they proved to be unfounded.

Cascarino impressed us during training and we played him in a full game on the training pitch against our best two centre halves, Stevie Bruce and Peter Shaw. The game went very well and as we walked off afterwards, Stevie Bruce came over and said, 'Where the fuck did you get him from? I wouldn't like to play against him every week.'

That decided it for us so we decided to sign him and opened negotiations with Crockenhill about the money. The boy wasn't under contract and when we talked about the price, the manager surprised us by saying that instead of receiving money, what they really needed was equipment. We offered him £500 to buy some but he didn't want the hassle of buying the kit so instead we agreed to give him twelve tracksuits and some new footballs. We also said we would play a pre-season friendly with Cascarino in Gillingham's team and Crockenhill could keep the receipts.

I heard from someone at Millwall that, when Bob Pearson of Millwall found out that we were going to sign Cascarino, Pearson made an offer of more money for him to join that team. When I asked Cascarino about this, he told me that he had turned down Millwall because he had already made a promise to Gillingham and intended to stick by his commitment. It's ironic that after I left Gillingham to go to Tottenham, Millwall bought Cascarino for, I understand, £225 000 and he went on to have a great career with Millwall, Chelsea and the Republic of Ireland.

Charlie Cox, the chairman of Gillingham, was a larger than life character, always looking for some scheme to help the club. His wife, Mary, was quite a character in her own right and could be quite outspoken. Mary was never one to hold back if she had an opinion, however outrageous it might be. Sometimes she would speak without much forethought. Charlie and Mary had a catering business under contract with some cricket clubs. One of their contracts was with the Kent County Cricket Club where, on one occasion, Mary had had a row with a couple of the Asian cricketers, who were Muslims.

Charlie told me about it. He came into my office at Gillingham one day, saying that Mary had served up pork sausages and pork pies at the subsequent Kent game. Fortunately, or unfortunately at least for Mary, someone must have rumbled that they were pork and an almighty rumpus broke out – again. Mary had told them they were beef sausages and maybe it had been a mistake but, seeing the way Charlie was laughing and knowing Mary as I did, it always seemed more likely that she had been getting her own back. She did tell me afterwards that she wasn't having foreigners telling her how to run her business. If that had happened today, she certainly would have been in deep trouble, whereas at that time they just lost the contract. Times change.

FAMILY MATTERS

I hadn't treated my wife Joyce as well as I should have. She did a fantastic job bringing the boys up while I was away in America and we stayed on good terms after the divorce, which she hadn't wanted. She found herself a good job with an American paper company and she was promoted quite quickly in the sales division. I provided for her and the boys financially but Joyce never demanded anything. Eventually she told me she had met someone else and then introduced me at a family gathering to her prospective new husband, Lionel. The boys were now young men and they told me they got on well with Lionel. I might not have been expected to get on with him myself as we were clearly quite different personalities, he being a gentle, reserved motor mechanic with his own business and interested in Formula 1 racing and me being somewhat louder, more outgoing and a football man.

Nevertheless we had a good relationship from the outset and I thought he was a better match for Joyce than I had been. My sister, Edie, even thought Lionel looked rather like my elder brother, Alfie, who had died of heart problems years earlier.

After Lionel and Joyce announced their wedding plans, I was talking to Lionel on his own one night at a night club in Sydenham, a watering-hole for some of the family, where I used to meet my sons. I was surprised when Lionel said, 'Why don't you come to our wedding reception?'

I said I would have to think about it but he encouraged me and said, 'You'll be more than welcome.'

I mentioned this to my sons and they both said, 'Are you sure he wasn't joking?' I believe they mentioned it to Joyce but she didn't expect me to turn up.

On the day of the wedding, given that it was at the end of the season when everything is reasonably quiet, I decided that I would go along to the reception, which was to be held in the night club, Twilights, in Sydenham. By early evening I expected the wedding meal to have been long finished and was expecting the guests to be gathered around the bar ready for the evening dance. I didn't know that the reception had overrun a bit and, instead of everyone being informally gathered around the bar, they were still sitting in their formal places at their tables with the speeches still to come.

Outside I could hear the noise within the room and I pushed open the double doors and strolled into the reception. Everything went suddenly quiet – you could have heard a pin drop. Then I heard a collective gasp from the guests as they all knew who I was and presumably were not expecting me, the ex-husband, to turn up at my ex-wife's wedding. I certainly wasn't out to cause trouble, having only come at Lionel's insistence and I was pleased to see Joyce happy again. I said, 'Good evening. I'm sorry I barged in. I'll be at the bar,' and turned to leave.

With that Vince came out and asked if I was all right, followed by Lionel, who insisted I was to stay for a drink, so I stayed on and we ended up having a great evening with all the family celebrating Joyce's wedding. We've stayed good friends ever since.

It was some time later that summer that I next misbehaved, when I was invited to a barbecue at the parents-in-law of my younger son, John. All of the family were invited, including Joyce and Lionel and me. When I arrived the proceedings were well underway and Lionel had volunteered to do the cooking. The barbecue was situated on a higher level of ground at the bottom of garden. There were steps leading up to it and Lionel was standing on the top behind the barbecue doing the cooking. It was a bright sunny day and Lionel was wearing a heavy protective apron and was obviously overheating, standing by the hot coals.

After a few drinks and a laugh with the boys and the relatives gathered there, I started to feel mischievous. I had already been told that Lionel liked a glass of whisky but that Joyce had warned in advance that he wasn't to have any. I walked over to Lionel, looking up at him from the lower area of ground. He had a glass of beer in his hand when I said to him 'Lionel. You look hot. Why don't you have a whisky?'

He said that he had better not. I turned round to Joyce who was standing nearby and said, 'If he enjoys a whisky, let him have just one.'

Joyce didn't argue with me and said it was OK, so I went to the other end of the garden where the optics were and prepared a drink for Lionel. I poured the whisky but then added a few others and my hand slipped on the other optics so he had a drop of everything in that drink. I shouted to Lionel, 'Do you want water with that,' and he said that would be fine so I topped the glass to the brim.

I took it up to him and left him enjoying his drink and tending to the barbecue. The weather was getting warmer all the time and I could see that Lionel was still looking hot and bothered. I walked up and asked him if the sausages were ready. With a slightly shaky hand, he put a couple on a disposable plate and leaned forward to hand me the plate. As I turned to go back to the boys, Lionel turned to the barbecue but lost his footing on the slope and did a double somersault backwards down the hill. He was lying on his back with his arms and legs in the air like an upturned beetle.

With that someone said, 'Lionel's down,' and they ran over to help him up.

We were creased up with laughter but Joyce was fuming and looked straight at me. 'How much whisky did you give him?' she demanded.

'Only one,' I said, but I avoided mentioning the other spirits that were mixed in with it. I might have got away with it but I was later grassed up by John's father-in-law, who reported to Joyce that he had seen me filling the glass. Fortunately Lionel wasn't hurt and he spent the rest of the afternoon sitting in the sunshine beside a big garden roller, which given the chance Joyce would probably have preferred to see flattening me.

Back at Gillingham, Keith had assembled quite a good squad of players. He had already signed David Shearer, a Scottish lad from Fort William and Terry Cochrane, from Middlesbrough, two real characters, who were best mates at the club and were always getting into escapades. My first clash with Dave came when I was leaving the ground one night to go off to a game. I drove through the centre of the village to get an evening paper and, when I pulled into the side of the road, I saw in a doorway something that looked like two down-and-outs.

I had to do a double take to recognise one of them as Dave Shearer and the other was certainly a tramp. Both had cans of beer. I went over to them and looked down at Dave. He couldn't believe it was me standing over him and I said, 'What the fucking hell are you doing here?'

He said he was helping this old man. 'Are you mad?' I asked. 'It's a small community in Gillingham and everybody supports the club. If anybody has seen you, the manager, you and the rest of the club will be in trouble with the press.' I pulled him to his feet, stood him against the wall. He was a bit of a hard player and I didn't know how he was going to react. I said, 'Now get yourself off home and don't you be late in the morning or you're in trouble.'

To be fair, he was one of the first to arrive in the morning. He looked at me and said in his soft Scottish brogue, 'Are you OK?'

I said, 'I will be if you can knock in a few goals on Saturday and I'll forget all about last night.'

There were a few more incidents with Terry Cochrane later on that did cause Keith Peacock a few headaches, but he was a good manager and a diplomat and managed to put the lid on their antics. One particular time after a game Shearer must have got a bit homesick and decided that he wanted to go back to Fort William. It's some distance from Gillingham to Fort William so he decided to borrow Terry Cochrane's car but without asking Terry first.

Unfortunately half way through his journey, somewhere up in the Midlands, he had a crash, possibly through lack of sleep, but at least he walked away from it uninjured. Keith was informed by the police, presumably because Dave had told them to inform the club. How Keith kept it out of the press I will never know. There must have been some forgiveness from Terry because they were best mates, but I do know the directors of Gillingham wanted to cancel Dave's contract because of his conduct. Keith, however, talked them around into keeping him. To be fair, Shearer respected that decision and appreciated what Keith had done for him. He and Terry were two great characters and, apart from their antics, were good lads and were both great players who gave their all on the pitch, so the crowd loved them. I haven't been in touch with either of them since I left Gillingham.

In 1985 I had been to a game at Swindon and when I arrived home in Peckham, there was a message on my answerphone from Peter Shreeves, then the manager of Tottenham. 'Are you going to the Sports Journalists' Association dinner tomorrow night?' he asked. 'If so, I'd like to have a chat with you. Let me know if you're going or not.' I phoned him back the next morning. His wife, Carol, answered as he was out so I told her not to worry him and confirmed that I would be at the dinner that night at the Hilton Hotel in Park Lane and I'd meet him in the bar.

I arrived quite early and sat waiting in the bar and to my surprise Peter came in with the Tottenham chairman, Irving Scholar. Peter introduced me and I really thought that they were going to enquire about buying Tony Cascarino, the lad we had brought to Gillingham from non-league Crockenhill Town. But they said nothing more at that moment. After the meal and in the interval before the comedian was due to come on I walked into the bar and there were Peter and Irving Scholar.

'Are you going to buy us a drink?' asked Peter.

'Yes, sure,' I said. 'Was there anything particular you wanted to ask me?'

'How would you like to come and work for us at Tottenham?' Irving asked.

I was taken back a little bit and hesitated before asking, 'As what?'

'To take over from Bill Nicholson,' said Peter.

'Are you sure?' I asked, thinking it must be a wind-up as Bill Nicholson was something of a legend.

But then Irving said that Bill was thinking about stepping down and added, 'We think you're the one who could take over his position.'

Right away, Peter started selling the club to me but in fact he didn't need to do that. I was thinking about all the big guns they had there at the time – Glenn Hoddle, Ossie Ardiles, Ray Clemence – a team full of internationals, even the likes of Paul Miller, an icon and a great favourite of the crowd, who I had known previously. Irving Scholar then discussed wages, which were double what I was then earning at Gillingham. I still had a year's contract to go but agreed right away to join Tottenham on the proviso that they would have to speak with the chairman at Gillingham, Charlie Cox.

I didn't know it at the time and didn't hear about it until much later but apparently, while Irving Scholar and Peter Shreeves were keen for me to join Tottenham, I had my detractors who thought I was not a big enough name to take over from Bill. One of these was Morris Keston, a season-ticket holder who had at one time been offered a directorship on the Tottenham board and who was very influential within the club, organising charity events and testimonials for the players. He was a high roller who spent time in Las Vegas and was friends with Frank Sinatra and his mates.

Morris had his doubts that I would be able to do the job and challenged Irving Scholar by asking what I could do for the club. Irving replied that I had a good eye for players and would spot talent. Fortunately for me, Irving and Peter won the day. Since then I have become good friends with Morris, who relayed these stories to me himself with the comment, 'We all make mistakes'.

I hardly slept that night. My adrenaline was running high. I arrived at the training ground at Gillingham the next morning and spoke briefly to Keith about the offer, adding that Tottenham would talk to them. Keith, a gentleman and a real professional, said, 'Well you've got nothing to think about. You've got to take it. I'll speak to Charlie.'

Charlie said that they needed compensation or I wouldn't be going anywhere so I said, 'Charlie, do me a favour. No disrespect but it's like going from Lyons Corner House to the Ritz.'

At the time, I wasn't getting on too well with Paul Taylor, the coach. I thought his attitude to the players wasn't right and he wasn't getting the best out of them. So perhaps it was time for me to go at any rate.

On the compensation front I said to Charlie and Keith, 'Surely you aren't going to spoil my chance if they won't pay whatever you want in compensation?' I added that John Gorman, who I had taken as one of my first signings to Tampa three years prior to that, had finished his time in the States and was looking for a job as a coach. John had done very well for us out in Tampa so I suggested that Keith let him take my job. I think he persuaded the chairman to do exactly that.

After that, everything was agreed. Keith got in touch with John and he took over from me at Gillingham so I was free to go to Tottenham. When I was working out terms with the financial director, Peter Day, at Tottenham, he asked if we had to negotiate the compensation and I said, 'No, it's all settled.'

He asked me if I expected a percentage of fees for any players bought or sold in deals that I initiated. I had never been asked that and my first thought was, 'I wonder if they're trying me out.'

I recalled that, after I had signed Washington Olivera from Uruguay to take the place of Rodney Marsh, Peter Taylor, the Nottingham Forest assistant to Brian Clough, had asked me in Tampa if I got a percentage of the fee if he were sold back. When I said I didn't, he had said, 'Well you're mad. You should have that put in your contract.'

But talking to Peter Day I said, 'No, I'm quite satisfied with what I'm getting.'

Even he said, 'Are you sure?'

'Yes that's fine,' I said. As the years went on I realised that it was all legitimate and I would probably have been a bit better off in my dealings in those eight years in Tottenham if I had been a bit more savvy but, no matter, I was quite happy with the deal I was offered. I was on my way.

FROM LYONS CORNER
HOUSE TO THE RITZ

And so began my eight great years at Tottenham from 1985 to 1993. On my first day at the training ground, the press were in evidence. Peter Shreeves introduced me to all the players and then we got involved with the warm-up and preparation to make us ready for the pre-season.

There was a five-a-side at the end of every session, which Peter loved and at the end of that first one he said, 'Do you want to have a play?'

I was a bit reluctant as I was in my early fifties and seeing all the talented big guns around, I didn't want to make myself look a mug. But Peter insisted, saying, 'It's a bonding issue,' so with that I joined in and in actual fact did quite well. I think the players appreciated the fact that I made the effort and possibly earned some respect as they hadn't known who I was previously.

Two of the lads wanted to have a bit of banter. They were the two hard men at the time, Paul Miller (better known as Maxi Miller, obviously after the old comedian Max Miller) and Graham Roberts, but they seemed to warm to me a little bit. Peter Shreeves had told the two of them, 'Don't mess with him because he shot people in Malaya.' They laughed and wanted to know all about that and seemed genuinely fascinated with some of the stories I told them.

A few weeks after that I got involved in another game after a training session, when I was in opposition to Ossie Ardiles.

Early on in the game I laid on a great ball, if I say so myself, for a winger called John Chiedozie and he scored. I think Ossie was quite impressed with that until I laid another ball towards Glenn Hoddle and the ball went straight out of play because my touch was too heavy. I put my hands up to acknowledge this and Ossie Ardiles walked over to me and said in his Argentinian accent, 'You have a touch like an elephant.'

A few of the lads laughed at that and I turned round to him and said light-heartedly, 'Another remark like that, Ossie, and they'll be another Falklands war.'

There was an awkward silence. Ossie turned his back on me and walked away, while Maxi Miller came over and said that Ossie had had a cousin killed in that war and it was a sensitive subject. So after the game I walked over to put my arm round Ossie's shoulder and said, 'Sorry, mate. I didn't mean any offence.'

'No problem,' he said. From then on we always got on OK and I had a lot of respect for Ossie.

Years later when Ossie had just been appointed to take over as manager at Tottenham from Ray Clemence and Dougie Livermore, who were in temporary charge after Terry Venables had left the club, Alan Sugar gave Ossie the job of giving me the news that I was being sacked. I thought at the time that if Sugar had had any guts he would have told me himself, not least as on his TV series these days he apparently has no hesitation in saying, 'You're fired!'

Instead, Ossie had to do the deed for him. He was very apologetic about it. It was the start of a new season and I had just come back from a holiday in Tampa. He called me in and said, 'I'm sorry, Ted. It's nothing to do with me but I have been told that your contract's up and won't be renewed.'

I said, 'Ossie, I know it's not your fault,' and with that we shook hands.

When I arrived at Tottenham, Peter Shreeves was the manager and John Pratt was his number two. Dougie Livermore was reserve team manager and John Moncur was the youth team academy manager. That first year didn't go so well as far as the team was concerned and we didn't do too well in the league, finishing in the bottom half. So after I had been there for one year, Peter and Johnny both got the sack.

I had just returned from a game near the end of the season when I got a call from Peter to say that he had been sacked and that David Pleat was coming in as manager, bringing with him his coach at Luton, Trevor Hartley, and very likely his chief scout, Ron Howard. If that was the case I might have got the elbow as well, as I said to Peter at the time.

But Peter said, 'I think you're going to be all right.' I asked why he thought that and he said, 'The vibes I've got from the chairman, Irving Scholar.'

'Well, Peter,' I said, 'you got me here to the club so maybe I should resign anyway.'

'Don't you dare do that,' he said. 'You've still got a contract. If you do that it won't entitle you to a penny and anyway I spoke to the chairman about you and Dougie Livermore.'

Knowing football as I did, I wouldn't have put too much faith in that. It was a shame that Peter got the sack because he was good to be around and always made things enjoyable. Maybe, as things turned out, he would have been better off as a number two or a coach as he did well when Terry brought him back into the fold in a coaching capacity.

No one ever told me what was to happen under Pleatie so I just carried on as before, not sure how long I was going to be in the job. I remember changing my answering machine message at home and it went something like, 'This is Ted Buxton. Hopefully I'm still chief scout at Tottenham. If I'm not here, leave a message.'

It was then that I got a message from David Pleat, to meet him at our new training ground. We shared it with a company, which wasn't ideal because at lunchtimes we also had to share the canteen, with space blocked off for us and the players after a training session. I already knew David quite well because while I was in Tampa Bay we had taken a player from him called David Moss, a winger and a very good player, and David had stayed in the Bay Harbour Hotel in Clearwater Beach where we spent some time together.

I remember the first words David had said to me when he arrived at Tottenham: 'I hear you are a bit of a Jack the Lad.'

'What are you on about?' I asked.

'Well, you're divorced.'

'So what's that got to do with it?'

'You've got a girlfriend and you stop over there sometimes,' he said.

That annoyed me and he knew it. 'Whatever you're hearing, it doesn't affect the job I do and you and everybody else should know that,' I said.

Later I got the distinct feeling that he wasn't too pleased that I had a close rapport with the players. On one occasion Paul Allen and Clive Allen came to me and were talking about the opposition in the game that was coming up at the next weekend. The two of them were always keen to know about the opponents they were up against and if I had any information that could help them during the game.

David Pleat rushed over in an agitated state and started saying, 'What are they talking about? Are they talking about me?'

'Do me a favour,' I said. 'Why would they want to talk about you? They were asking me about the next game and what I thought about the opposition.'

'I don't want them to keep coming over and talking to you,' said David.

So I said, 'You'd better tell them then.' I think perhaps they preferred to talk to me rather than his number two, Trevor Hartley, who it seemed was never too popular with the players.

Anyway the pre-season started and it was then that David called me into his office. 'Who's the best centre half that you've seen who might be available?' he asked.

'Richard Gough at Dundee United,' I said.

To my surprise he replied, 'That's a good shout.'

We signed Richard and it turned out that he had a bigger opinion about how the game should be played than either Paul (Maxi) Miller or Graham Roberts and would let it be known in no uncertain terms if the coaching staff or anybody else under-achieved. Later on when we had a bit of blip in a couple of games and we weren't playing too well, Pleatie said, 'I want all the players in the middle of the pitch in the centre circle and we'll try to sort out between ourselves what's been going wrong.' Pleatie looked round at everyone and added, 'I want to hear if anybody has got anything to say.'

With that, Goughie got up, pointed a finger at Pleatie's number two, Trevor Hartley, and said loudly, 'That's our problem. It's him, He's fucking useless.'

The meeting was abandoned very quickly.

Pleatie's first season didn't start too well but then he decided to change the system. He went with a 4–5–1 formation with Clive Allen on his own up front supported by Ossie Ardiles, Glenn Hoddle, Tony Galvin, Paul Allen and Steve Hodge. It turned out to be a great success, with Clive Allen scoring forty-nine goals backed up by goals from Ardiles, Galvin and Hoddle.

We finished third in the league and reached the cup final against Coventry in the 1986–87 season. Considering the start we had had it was quite an achievement. We started favourites for the final versus Coventry, which was managed by my good friend John Sillett, who was an ex-Chelsea player, fondly known as Schnozzle for obvious reasons. We are still good friends; we meet up at race meetings and he often phones because he owns a few horses and likes to give me a chance of winning a few bob. Unfortunately, we lost 3–2 so it wasn't the best of days, although we had enough chances. We hadn't played too well. Gary Mabbutt scored a goal for us but then, unfortunately put in an own goal to give Coventry the game. Coventry later celebrated Gary Mabbutt's knee.

Gary suffered from diabetes and had to inject himself regularly each day. His condition was well managed but to make sure that his blood sugar levels didn't get too low, the medical staff always arranged to have biscuits and fruit drink available around the pitch. The only time we had a problem was a few years later when Paul Gascoigne had joined us from Newcastle and Terry Venables had taken over from David Pleat. While Terry was taking a training session, Gary started to wobble and his eyes were glazing over. It was clear that his sugar level had dropped so Dougie Livermore and I called for the biscuits and fruit drinks. No biscuits or drinks could be found so when we asked where they had gone, Gazza piped up that he had eaten them. No one had told him about Gary and he thought the refreshments were for the team.

Panic stations ensued until Roy Reyland, the kitman, sprinting like a Road Runner, raced back to the medical room and produced a Mars bar and drinks. Gazza was still perplexed and couldn't understand how anyone with such a condition could be a professional footballer. So after that session, he went into the changing room and saw Gary giving himself an insulin injection. Gazza was apologetic and asked Gary how many times a day he had to inject himself.

'Three times a day,' said Gary.

'How long for?' asked Gazza.

'For life,' said Gary.

'Fuck me. I'd rather be dead,' was Gazza's reply.

At the end of David Pleat's second season he said we had to negotiate my new contract and indicated that he wanted to cut my wages as he thought I earned too much. I thought there was some ulterior motive because I thought he probably wanted to bring in Ron Howard, who had been with him at Luton. I said to David, 'If I have to take a cut I think you should do as well.'

'I can't do that,' he said.

'Nor can I,' I replied. By then I was getting a bit heated and I think he could sense that.

'Think about it over the weekend and we'll meet on Monday at 11.00 in the office at White Hart Lane,' he said in a more placatory tone.

At 6 a.m. on Monday morning, Johnny Moncur, our youth development officer, phoned me. 'John, what the hell are you doing calling me at 6 o'clock in the morning?' I asked.

He said simply, 'Go and get the *Sun*.'

I promptly got dressed and went to get the paper to find, splashed across the front page, a terrible photo of David Pleat with a story that he had been pulled over by the police in a red light district. David, I understand, claimed that he was merely asking directions. Pity we didn't have satnav in those days.

I drove into White Hart Lane. As I walked into the reception, I saw that the girls around the office had plastered copies of the newspaper all around the office. I immediately made them take them down. I waited until about 10 a.m. and then phoned David's house. His wife, Maureen, answered the phone, sounding distressed. I said that I had arranged to meet David at 11 a.m. to which she replied that she hadn't seen him all night.

So I said, 'When you hear from him, tell him that I'm here waiting for him,' adding that if I heard any news I would ring her straight away.

Half an hour later I got a call from Irving, the chairman. He said, 'Could you meet me and the rest of the directors at my office in Grosvenor Square. I've got David here with me and I would like you to come and pick him up and take him home.'

'Can you phone his wife?' I asked.

He said it had already been done and that his car was still at Grosvenor Square. He asked me to arrange to have it picked up. I got hold of Gerry Lambert, our security man, and arranged for him to go and pick the car up to take it back to the club. When I walked into the chairman's office, there was a strange atmosphere. Both the chairman and the directors thanked me for coming. I asked where David was and he was sitting in a big arm chair in the office looking absolutely shattered. Although I felt a brief moment of satisfaction, given what had previously gone between us, I felt sympathetic, especially when he got off the chair, took my hand and said, 'Thank you, Ted, I knew I could rely on you.' Ironic, I thought.

I drove him home. I had never been to his bungalow in Luton before. As we drove into his road, there were masses of photographers blocking the entrance to his driveway. He was shaken at the sight. I said, 'Don't worry, David. I'll drive straight towards them into your drive. You just jump out and I'll sort them out.'

As we drove in and I moved the photographers out of the way, his front door was already open and Maureen was standing there, so he got out of the car and rushed in. They were firing questions at him as he was went and as I followed him I turned round and said, 'Fuck off lads and give him a break.'

For the following week I ferried him around and looked after him and things got back to normal. We started to become good friends then and I found myself enjoying his company. I think he liked having me around after that.

At the start of the next season, David phoned me a week before we were due to report for the pre-season. 'Ted, I want you at the training ground early on Thursday,' he said.

So I got there on time. He and Trevor Hartley were in the recreation room with Gerry Lambert. He and Trevor were sitting at a desk and beside that was another small table with a chair.

David said, 'When the players get here, that's where I want you to sit.'

When the players started to arrive they took their places. We still had most of the big names then. David said, 'I hope you all had a good break and, first, I want you to get in your minds that you have to respect your wife and your families and whatever has gone on is history and if any of you have any problems I want you to go to Ted. He's the new troubleshooter.'

I was as shocked as the players when he said that as he had never even mentioned it to me. A few cheers went up from the players and I think it was Paul Miller who shouted out 'Troubleshooter Buxton.' That brought a smile to David and Trevor's faces so for a few days I was known as 'TS'.

The pre-season started quite well. Dougie Livermore was now reserve team coach. Ray Clemence had retired and was now goalkeeping coach but still had a player's contract in case the goalkeepers were injured. One of our first games in the season was Middlesbrough. They had a pre-season friendly and David decided that he and I would check out the shape of the team and their tactics. We shared the driving up to Middlesbrough. About an hour into the journey with David driving, we stopped and had a bit of refreshment. He told me to make sure I looked after the players. 'If you have any big problems come to me but if you can sort it out, do it.'

We got back in the car with him still in the driver's seat. I asked if he wanted to swap over, and he said he would go for another half-hour. In that half-hour, he asked me about my private life, my family and my divorce and I explained to him that everything was fine. I was still on good terms with Joyce, my ex-wife, and my two boys, Vince and John, had settled down.

Then he came out with, 'I've been told that you fought in the Malayan campaign.'

'That's right,' I said.

'Were you ever frightened?' he asked.

'I don't think so,' I said.

'I heard you killed people out there.'

'Well, of course,' I said. 'It was a communist uprising because Malaya belonged to Britain and most of the rubber plantation owners were British so we had to defend them and the tin-mine owners.'

'How did you feel when you shot people?' he asked.

'It wasn't just me, we were a platoon that shot people,' I said. 'You don't think about it. The adrenaline just flows and you get on with it because that's what you're there for. All eighteen-year-olds serving our country. In a strange sort of way it's like scoring a goal, you just focus on what you have to do.'

'Did you feel sorry for them?' he asked.

'Not really, David, but there are some people in this country that I would get more pleasure shooting than I did them,' I said.

With that he nearly went off the road. He pulled over and I took over the driving after that.

A RUMBUSTIOUS LIFE

After losing in the Cup Final to Coventry at the end of the season, David's personal difficulties resurfaced and he left Tottenham. Rumours were rife that Terry Venables was being brought in from Barcelona. One league game after the Cup Final, we were playing Aston Villa when I got a call from Irving Scholar to say that he would like me to go with Trevor Hartley and the team to Aston Villa. I was a bit surprised that I was included but then I got a call from Trevor himself saying he had had a call from David even though he had already left the club, telling Trevor that Trevor should take me with him.

We didn't play too well at Aston Villa. We were down at half time and in the dressing room players such as Ossie, Glenn Hoddle and Richard Gough were all looking for something to inspire them, because everybody had taken a knock-back after losing the Cup Final when we had been favourites to win.

So when Trevor sat the lads down I could feel the tension in the team. I don't think Trevor did himself any favours by spouting off about the England cricket team that had just won a test match, especially as it was the start of the cricket season and thus the end of the football season. The footballers should take the lead of the cricketers, he said.

I could see the players' heads were down and they weren't paying a blind bit of notice. There was a pause as Trevor waited for a response and none was forthcoming. I decided to say something. 'I can't believe we are down to this mob because there is not one player out there that could get into our side and there's not one of their players that I would swap for any of you,' I yelled.

One or two voices said, 'Yes, you're right. Let's go for it.'

With that there was a lot of handclapping from the team. As we trooped out of the dressing room, we passed Irving, who must have been just out of sight behind the door and had heard the half time chat. I nodded to him and said, 'Afternoon, Chairman.'

He had a brief word with Trevor. Unfortunately for Trevor, he was fired a few days later. It was then announced that Terry Venables was the new manager of Tottenham Hotspur and was bringing in his number two at Barcelona, Allan Harris, who had been with Terry for a number of years.

Allan was a great lad to be with and he was good fun. Of course I had known him and his brother Ronnie (Chopper) Harris from their Chelsea days. Ronnie used to come down to watch me coach at Epsom and Ewell. I wasn't sure whether Terry would keep me on because he had his own staff and there was a lot of talk in the papers that he would bring in his old chief scout at Queens Park Rangers, Arnie Warren. So I was bit apprehensive when I received a call from Terry asking me to meet him at Enfield on the Cambridge Road and take him to the training ground. He said we would have a chance to have a chat en route.

During the drive, he asked me about the players and the pitfalls and I began to feel we had the same ideas and a rapport. At the training ground, Terry noted a number of changes that were needed to be made to the ground and raised these with Irving Scholar. The more I saw of the way Terry worked, the keener I was to work with him. I had the strong impression that, if he had wanted to get rid of me, he would have said so early on but I wanted to be clear on where I stood so the following day when we met up at the club, I asked him outright if he was planning to bring in anyone else.

'No, you've got no worries there,' he said, and so began my fourteen-year period working with Terry, which was to take me to the England national team, Portsmouth and Crystal Palace. We went for a drink together later that day and over a few drinks we discovered that we had a similar sense of humour, sharing banter and stories about his time in Barcelona and my time in America.

When Terry first came to Tottenham he decided to send the players and staff for a bonding session in Porto Banus in Spain and put Allan Harris and me in charge of the trip together with Roy Reyland, the kitman, and John Sheridan, the physio. We had a lovely hotel, where the management was very welcoming, but a number of incidents occurred during the trip that meant it wasn't the best of bonding sessions.

First, we sussed out the bars around Porto Banus. The first one that Allan Harris had checked out was run by Shirley Bassey's son. It was a nice champagne-type of bar with a pianist and singer, but while we were there, there were girls floating in and out of the bar into the back room and coming out later and we started to wonder what that was about. But we didn't ask any questions.

The entertainers were a man playing the piano and a lady, who was a good singer, giving us all the decent ballads. One of lads said, 'Go on, Ted, get up and give us a song.'

Allan Harris added, 'Why don't you give the girl a break?'

So after a few glasses of wine, we asked the pianist if it would be OK and he said it was fine. So he asked what I wanted to sing. 'What about Sinatra's *All The Way*,' I asked, so with a tinkle on his piano he was off.

I got right into the song. The lady singer was sitting by the pianist, so I moved towards her, took her by the hand, got hold of her and started singing to her. The song ran 'When somebody loves you…' and ends with '… I love you, all the way.' She was quite responsive: she was snuggling up to me and the boys were all geeing everybody up. I noticed the pianist wasn't too happy and, after the song finished, while the lads were shouting, 'More, more, another song, Ted', the piano player was definitely annoyed.

He took the lady by the arm and said, 'That's it, lads. We're finished for the night.'

As they left, one of the barmen called me over and said, 'He gets a bit wound up when anyone gets too close to her. She's his wife.' Oops.

During our stay I had a run-in with Mitchell Thomas, the left back from Luton Town we had signed in the David Pleat days. He was a bit of a rascal in that he liked practical jokes and it was one of these jokes that nearly got him killed – by me. John Sheridan, our physio, was a lovely man who did anything the players asked, which wasn't a good policy because whenever they needed extra training in the afternoons, he would tend to let them off. John as a young lad had suffered a horrific injury which left him with a damaged hip and a stiff leg. His knowledge was second to none but the players took advantage of his affliction and his good nature.

One afternoon we were all relaxing in the hotel. I was in my room waiting for a phone call from my son, Vince, on the birth of his first baby, which was due that day. On my balcony I saw a black arm with a bucket full of water coming round the veranda and then the bucket of water splashed all over me. Right away I knew that it was Mitchell and started shouting obscenities. At that moment Vinny Samways, one of the first-team players, shot out of my wardrobe and made for the door. I think the mood I was in must have worried him.

I chased after Mitchell and just as he was climbing back onto the balcony of John Sheridan's room, next to mine, I grabbed his leg. It was wet from all the water and it slipped out of my hand, which was just as well as I had every intention of chucking him over the balcony, which wouldn't have been a good idea because we were four floors up. He escaped through John's room, leaving me to go mad with John because he had allowed them to get into my room via his room and balcony.

I went looking for Vinny. I knew he was in one of the lad's rooms. I thought it might be Phil Gray's, a young Irish international, but the door was locked so I rammed it. At that moment Phil came along with another young player, Paul Moran, whose birthday was coming up the next day; they saw me along the corridor and ran for their lives when they saw the mood I was in. I got back into my room just as the phone was ringing and it was my son, Vince, to say that his son Jack had been born. That calmed me down and I went out with Allan Harris, Roy Reyland and John Sheridan, who was very apologetic. The players involved kept well away from me that night.

The next morning it was a beautiful day and I walked out onto my balcony and looked down on all the players having their breakfast below. Every player looked up, knowing what had gone on the day before. Mitchell looked up and said, 'Are you alright, Ted?'

I looked down at him and seeing he was sitting next to Vinny I said, 'No. I'm coming down to see you two now.' I went downstairs.

Allan Harris had come downstairs beside me and said, 'Come on, calm down.'

I looked at Mitchell and Vinny and said, 'Over there, you two, behind those trees and I'll sort you out and see if you're brave enough now.'

'It was only a joke,' said Mitchell.

'Not for me it wasn't,' I responded. 'I was waiting for an important phone call.'

'If you hit me, I'm going to sue you,' said Vinny.

'If you have enough fucking breath left,' I replied.

Later when we returned home and Allan and I met up with Terry, he had already heard about the incident with Mitchell and he said to me in all seriousness, 'You do realise that, without any doubt, if you had hit Mitchell or Vinny, I would have had to sack you.'

'No you wouldn't, Tel,' I replied.

There was a pause. 'Why?' he eventually asked.

'Because I would have been banged up for murder,' I said. With that, Terry and Allan both burst out laughing.

In the event Allan had acted as the peacemaker and had stepped in to calm down the situation. We had all shaken hands again at dinner that night and we went on to have a good week, but there was more to come.

Another incident arose when the management of the hotel complained to Allan and me that the younger players on the floor above us had been lobbing oranges at the staff who were having their break round the pool. The players involved were Phil Gray, Paul Moran and Mark Robson (who I signed from Exeter City as a young lad and is now an established coach). When asked to identify them, the manager described them as 'big fellows' but none of the three that we knew were involved were particularly tall. I also suspected that they were geed up by Mitchell and Vinny.

Coincidentally, John Sheridan was due to fly home early, two days before the rest of the team, to accompany Erik Thorstvedt, our goalkeeper, who was scheduled to have an operation on his knee. Whenever any of the players had medical treatment, especially important operations, John always attended to oversee the treatment. This gave Allan an idea about how to sort out the issue with the hotel management over the oranges incident. He called John in with me and told him that we were going to blame him for chucking the oranges and were going to tell the hotel manager that we were sending John home for misconduct.

John was a gentleman and certainly the last person you would find getting involved in an incident like orange throwing or misbehaving so he was not too happy, not least as he said, that Terry might assume he was to blame. Allan assured him that Terry wouldn't get to hear of it, but I am sure that Terry would have seen the funny side of it.

So we told the hotel manager that we had found the culprit and we were sending him home. The manager protested, saying, 'I didn't want it to go that far,' but Allan was very convincing, saying that we couldn't tolerate bad behaviour from the staff or players and we had to make an example to the rest. Later that day John and Erik were ready to leave and had their bags packed and standing beside them at the top of the steps outside the foyer.

Allan started loudly remonstrating with John, telling him that he couldn't tolerate any more of that behaviour, that he was being sent home because of the incident and then started kicking the bags down the stairs shouting, 'Go on. Off you go and I'll see you when we get back.'

I was with Alan, trying to keep a straight face and the players were all up on their balconies above watching this, creased up with laughter. One shouted out, 'Good riddance for getting us into trouble'.

Whilst the hotel manager and his deputy had apologised to me and Allan saying that they hadn't wanted it to go that far, Allan insisted, 'we have to nip these things in the bud and we don't tolerate this sort of behaviour by staff or players.' Allan's performance was so over the top that I still laugh remembering the incident.

Then there was Paul Moran's birthday. I think it was his twentieth. Terry Fenwick, one of our senior internationals, already famous for playing for England in the Maradona 'hand of God' game, arranged to hire a room for the night in a local bar. So we had a private room for all the players and invited any of the Brits on holiday to join us for a fee. Terry put a minder on the door, with one of the players taking the money.

All was going well when two big fellas walked up to the bar and got into conversation with a blonde lady. She had either paid to come in or had been let in for nothing, knowing the lads. Five minutes later a heavy-built man came in, said something to the two men and suddenly grabbed the blonde woman, slapped her and started dragging her out. Seeing this, Paul Moran, who was a skinny lad at the time, jumped up and said to Fenwick and to me, 'Let's sort these guys out and get them out of here.'

Fenwick turned to me and said, 'Is he sure?'

'Why?' I asked.

'You can't get mixed up with that mob,' Fenny told me and Paul Moran. 'That's Freddie Foreman.' I hadn't recognised him but anyone coming from South London, as I did, knew that Freddie Foreman was involved with the Kray twins and you didn't mess with him.

Freddie gave us an open hand gesture and said, 'No problems.' With that he left, with the girl and the two guys. We had a good night after that, celebrating Paul's birthday, but I wonder if he would have got to enjoy his next birthday if Fenwick hadn't realised who he was about to take on and stopped him.

Terry was building up a good squad, bringing in the likes of Chris Waddle from Newcastle United, Gary Lineker from Barcelona and Paul Stewart from Blackpool. And now, back in England, as part of the club health programme, Terry and I had to go to a medical centre in London's Gray's Inn Road for a BUPA check-up. All went well for the two of us until the last doctor we saw examined my prostate and told me that I might have a problem in a few years. It wasn't cancerous but the doctor recommended I see a consultant to have it sorted out.

An appointment was made for me in Harley Street and at the end of the season I was admitted for three days to have a small op. Everything went well and I had plenty of visitors. Terry came in and Eric Hall sent me a bottle of champagne, which I shared with a couple of the nurses, who came by after they came off duty to help me drink it.

The weeks that followed included several check-ups and I was told that it had gone very well but, before I could be signed off, they had to do one final test. The specialist said that I had to have an injection into my penis to make sure that no blood was leaking. He said that it was like a bee sting and that if I got an erection that would be a sure sign that everything was fine.

As soon as I had the injection, it went up like a rocket. 'Fine,' he said, 'see you in a month.' When he left the room, a nurse came in and said I would need a water test to see if the flow was OK. I looked at her and pulled down my tracksuit bottoms. She didn't turn a hair and just said that I could come back another time for the water test. She told me that it would go down in an hour or two but, if not, to come back promptly.

I drove home and five hours later I was still as hard as a rock. It was now becoming very uncomfortable. I rang the clinic and I was told to come back immediately. I left my house in South London, wearing a tracksuit as that was loose enough to hide my predicament. As I made my way to the clinic, I reached Vauxhall Bridge, where there was a fair bit of traffic. It was now over six hours since the injection but, as I sat there waiting in the queue, it started to relax and to my relief it went down completely.

I crossed the bridge and decided to go to 'Scribes', the nightclub Terry had bought in Kensington High Street, to see if Terry was around. When I walked in he was with Jimmy Tarbuck and Michael Parkinson as they had just been doing an interview. Terry was not too happy seeing me in a tracksuit until I told them what had happened. We had a good laugh and obviously there was a lot of banter about my 'Vauxhall Bridge' experience. As I was leaving, Michael Parkinson asked if the injection I had had was available in tablet form and I said they would make a fortune if it were. He must have seen the future because later on Viagra came out and must have made that fortune.

One of the funniest stories about John Sheridan was when ITV were doing an interview with Terry soon after his arrival at Tottenham. The camera crew wanted to film Terry going about his daily routine in the club. Terry had told me to get in early. The camera crew had set up in his office at the training ground. They were facing the doorway. Terry was at his desk beside the camera crew and they told me I was to walk in normally.

Terry would ask me to update him on the players, discuss who was in the treatment room and give him a rundown on the scouts who had been out assessing the teams we were due to play and to report on individual players. The interviewer said all I had to do was come into the room, talk to Terry and ignore the camera crew as if they were not there. He emphasised that I was not to look at the camera.

So I went out, came back in and Terry asked me his normal questions and I responded. Then Terry said, 'I need John Sheridan to let me know about any injuries in the team, so pop over and tell John where we are.' Off camera he told me to fill him in about not looking at the camera and to tell him just to act normally. So off I went and briefed John and then went back to Terry's room where I sat beside him. Five minutes later, John knocked at the door and came in. He said, 'Good morning, boss,' and looked straight into the camera lens with a big grin on his face.

Terry asked me, 'Didn't you tell him not to look at the camera?'

'Of course. I explained everything to him,' I said.

'Sorry, he did tell me that,' John chipped in.

'OK, John, go out and start again because it's getting late and we've got to get out to start training.'

With that John went out again. The camera man shouted 'OK, come in'.

John knocked at the door, came in and this time looked straight at the camera as he smiled broadly and said, 'Morning, boss.' We had another shot at it and the same thing happened. The whole episode was beginning to look like a Peter Sellers farce.

After the third time, I was finding it hard to keep a straight face but Terry was now starting to get agitated. He said, 'I tell you what we'll do. You go back to the treatment room and I'll come over to you and ask you the question there. Don't look at the camera.'

So John limped back to the treatment room, followed by Terry and the camera crew. This time they positioned the camera behind John with Terry talking to him, facing the camera so John couldn't look at the camera without turning right round. I had a bit of banter with several of the players to keep the scene realistic and this time John didn't get another chance to get it wrong, so they finally shot the scene. Even then as the camera crew filmed Terry and me walking out, John still managed to shoot around into camera view giving a big smile into the camera. I suspect they cut that from the final edit.

Later that day Terry and I had a drink together at the Carlton Tower Hotel. Over a glass of wine we shared a good laugh, reliving the day's events and raised a glass to John for the memorable day he had given us.

GAZZA

During this period in 1988 the spotlight was on Paul Gascoigne because he seemed to have everything. He was regarded as the Wayne Rooney of his day but, if he had been more mentally disciplined, Gazza could have gone further. And judging by his tactical awareness and the ability he displayed in encouraging the younger players, he could have been one hell of a coach. I used to say he had three lungs – he could run all day; he had balance, control, two good feet and was good in the air.

In my opinion he was a football genius, but there was a fine line between genius and madness. At heart he was the most generous person I have ever known. He was then at Newcastle under Jack Charlton, and Tottenham, like many other clubs, was aware of his ability and knew that he would become available. I went and watched him a few times and said to Terry, 'The boy's got everything.'

I think the fee at the time was over £2 million. Apparently, while we were negotiating with him, Alex Ferguson was also negotiating with him to join Manchester United. Gazza had veered between Manchester United and Tottenham and I believe Irving Scholar, our chairman, was well into negotiations when Gazza asked if there was any chance of getting his mum and dad's house redecorated and furnished. While Manchester United was still negotiating, Gazza would come back and say, 'Can my sister have a new fridge put into her house?' and requested one or two other domestic items for other relations. Each time Irving Scholar agreed and in the end, after all these extra bits and pieces, Gazza signed for Tottenham instead of for Alex Ferguson. That was Gazza, always thinking about other people and looking after them.

I remember talking to Jack Charlton and asking him about Gazza's character. Jack said, 'The boy will hopefully be a genius and could be a world-class player, but he's as nutty as a fruit cake. I've kicked his arse a few times and warned him about his future if he didn't straighten himself out.' When Gazza came down to Tottenham he warmed to Terry, and Terry certainly got the best out of him but the stories that surround Gazza and his schoolboy pranks and antics are legendary.

One of my first encounters with Gazza was coming away from the training ground one day and as I was walking to go back with Roy Reyland, the kitman, Gazza drew alongside me in his brand-new Merc and said, 'Do you want a lift, Ted? I'll take you back.'

As soon as I got in the car, I couldn't even get my seat belt on before he roared off at about nought to sixty in six seconds, but the trouble was that there were sleeping policemen all along the road out of the training ground. He hit every one going at speed, got into the main road and barely slowed down. When we got to the ground at White Hart Lane, he skidded round the car park, looked at me and said 'Weren't you scared?'

'Gazza,' I said, 'I have had to duck fucking bullets. Why should I be worried about a little car drive?'

'Oh, you're boring,' he said, and that was Gazza. Perhaps after that he appreciated that I wasn't someone to mess around with but it never stopped him having a go at certain times.

Another incident with a vehicle occurred when we were heading for a game against Nottingham Forest. The kitman had stacked all the kit ready for loading onto the minibus to take the team to the main coach, which was waiting at White Hart Lane to take us to the game. A couple of traffic cones were standing beside the pile of kit and it didn't take Gazza long to grab one of the cones.

He climbed up on the minibus with a traffic cone and lodged in on the top of the roof rack. John Cobberman was one of the regular drivers for the players and used to drive the players around to look at new houses when they joined the club. Gazza always tormented John but John took it all in good part and enjoyed being involved with the players.

John spotted the traffic cone and was climbing up onto the roof of the minibus to retrieve it, when Gazza jumped into the bus and started driving off. John threw the cone to the ground and shouted out, 'Gazza, let me get off.'

Gazza accelerated and drove out of the ground onto the main road, heading for the A1. John was now clinging on for dear life. Gazza shot down to the end of the road, came round a roundabout and came back again with John still hanging on to the roof rack, shouting out with his legs swinging all over the place. He looked like Norman Wisdom doing one of his comedy stunts. Gazza screeched to a halt and John slid down, white as a sheet. 'That's set me up for the day,' Gazza told John.

'You nearly gave me a heart attack,' John replied.

Another night John had driven Gazza to a function and afterwards took him back to his hotel. Gazza then invited John to stay and have a drink with him and a few friends in his hotel room. John had a bit too much to drink and fell asleep on the bed. Gazza then went into the bathroom, got shaving foam and a razor and shaved off one of John's eyebrows. John didn't realise anything had happened until he woke hours later and looking in the mirror saw what Gazza had done.

I think Gazza started to appreciate me one afternoon when everyone had left the training ground and he was left on his own. He never liked being alone and always seemed to need people around him. He came up to the office where I was. I was going off to a game that night straight from the training ground. He came in and said, 'Has the gaffer gone?' meaning Terry.

'Yeh, he has,' I said.

'Would you mind if I had a bit of target practice?' he asked.

'What are you on about?' I asked.

He said he had a licensed rifle in the boot of his car and wanted to do some target practice. As you looked out of the coaching window across the ground, there was a row of houses overlooking the training ground enclosed by an eight foot wall. Gazza said, 'I'm going to put a couple of bottles out along the wall and shoot them off the wall.'

I said, 'Gazza, you can't do that because those are people's gardens and you'll be in trouble.'

'What about if I put them down on the floor our side?' he asked.

'Go on then,' I said, because I needed to get him out of the way and pacify him. So up he came with his rifle and promptly hit one of the bottles first time, with no problem.

'How about that then,' he asked.

'Yeh, quite impressive, Gazza,' I said.

With that he ran down and put up two or three more bottles on the ground and raced back up to me and said, 'Do you want to have a go?'

I did and I hit two of the bottles straight off. He looked at me and said, 'How did you learn to shoot like that?'

'Gazza, we had to shoot at real people in Malaya,' I said.

'Where's Malaya?' he asked.

'Gazza, when we were eighteen we had to go into the army and fight,' I said. He looked a bit puzzled as I don't think he'd had any idea about that, but after that I seemed to have his full attention, whatever I said to him.

Apart from his antics he was a child at heart really. One with a big heart. For instance, we used to have people from the rag trade come down with suits and trousers, selling everything. The guy with the suits said to me one day, 'I've got a lovely jacket to fit you,' because he knew Terry had opened up his nightclub Scribes and I had done quite a bit of singing there when the up-market karaoke started at 11.00 p.m. at night after the meal. It was a private club and not everyone could get in so we used to have a few celebs coming along.

'You'd look great singing in that,' said the guy. I said that I was going to have a shower and would come back and try it on, which I promptly did.

'Yes, this is for me,' I said 'Keep it for me. I'll be back in a minute and give you a cheque. How much is it?'

He said it was £120, as opposed to the normal price of £200. I said, 'Right you've got a deal.'

Gazza was already there picking out suits. He had picked out about three or four for his brothers, mates, uncles and whoever – all for his family and friends, and a couple of pairs of trousers for himself. I took the cheque back to the fellow made out for £120. He looked at me and said, 'It's all paid for.'

I asked what he was on about and he said, 'Gazza has already paid for it, with all the other things he has bought.'

I said, 'No, no, don't you do that. Hang on a minute.'

He said, 'He's already paid it.'

I went into Gazza who was sitting with a towel around him as he'd just had a hot bath. I said, 'Gazza, I can't let you do that, buying me a jacket.'

'It's too late I've already done it,' he said.

'I know that but I want to give you the 120 quid,' I said.

'If you do that, I'll give it to someone else or burn it,' he said.

'Gazza, I don't know what to say,' I said.

He said, 'Say nothing. It's my present to you.'

'What for?' I asked.

'You're a mate 'cos you got me here.' And that was Gazza at his best.

As well as John Sheridan, we had another physio, Dave Butler. Because of John's disability, it was agreed between them that

Dave would normally be the first to run onto the pitch to treat the players. John would stay on the bench until needed and would handle treatments off the pitch.

Terry had decided that that was the best arrangement after several incidents when Gazza would drop down on the far side of the pitch from the bench after he had taken a minor knock. He would wait until John had covered almost the full size of the pitch before he would jump up and say, 'I'm OK.' That was Gazza's sense of humour but John would then have to walk round the pitch to get back to the bench every time.

At the start of the next season we had a game against Chelsea. Three players went down, two from Chelsea and one of ours. They all needed attention so Chelsea's single physio had gone out, Dave Butler had already gone to our lad and John had jumped up, grabbed his bag and started limping across the pitch to help the second Chelsea player.

The crowd of nearly 30000 started chanting, 'They've got a problem – even their physio's injured,' and all started clapping John as he left the pitch. He loved it and responded by waving to the crowd. That was typical John, able to overcome his disability and earn a good living despite it. Years later he had a hip replacement and I don't believe he limps anymore.

David Beckham had come to Tottenham as a fourteen-year-old and we hoped to sign him on a pro-contract. Instead, he chose to sign with Manchester United where Malcolm Fidgeon was one of their scouts and had told Alex Ferguson about him.

Subsequently, Beckham claimed that Terry had not been particularly interested in signing him, but Johnny Moncur, the Tottenham youth team director, always said we were fighting a losing battle because his dad, Ted Beckham, wanted him to go north, as he was a big Manchester United fan. It must have been the right decision for David because he could not have topped the career he has had since with Manchester United and with

England and the other top clubs he has played for, as well as being an ambassador for the Olympics and for football.

I already knew Harry Redknapp, from my time in the US when Harry had been playing for the Seattle Sounders and I got to know him better when I regularly went to check out players at West Ham, where he was now manager with Frank Lampard Snr, his number two. Harry and Frank were brothers-in-law and, while Harry's son, Jamie, had been brought into Tottenham's youth side by John Moncur, Frank's son, Frank Jnr, was in the West Ham squad.

Frank Lampard Jnr was taking a bit of stick from the West Ham crowd because, as a midfield player, he wasn't doing enough box-to-box running. After one game, when I was having a glass of wine with Harry and Frank Snr, I suggested to them both that young Frank would do better if they encouraged him to concentrate on breaking beyond their main strikers in the attacking third, rather than focusing on defence. This subsequently became the style of play most associated with him. Terry Venables and I both thought then that Frank Jnr and Jamie Redknapp had the potential to become international players, which they did of course.

Since then Frank Jnr has gone on to become a world-class player. It was unfortunate that Jamie sustained a bad knee injury that reduced the number of caps I am sure he would have been able to win.

WINDS OF CHANGE

In the run up to the 1991 FA Cup Final, we had beaten Oxford United and Notts County. Arsenal had got through to the semi-final and, because both teams would attract a big crowd, it was decided for the first time to hold the semi-final at Wembley. It was a sell-out. The atmosphere was electric. The noise inside the stadium was something I had never experienced before. The crowd was wildly excited, not only by the two clubs' rivalry and the fact it was the first time the semis had been held in Wembley, but, because George Graham, the Arsenal manager, and Terry were best mates having played together at Chelsea. So you can imagine what banter there was going on between the teams, the managers and the groups of fans.

Both of my sons were at the game and I had brought them down onto the pitch before the crowds came in. I felt proud to be able to have our photos taken together just outside the tunnel at Wembley on such a special day. They were back in their seats when Ray Clemence, our goalkeeping coach, Dougie Livermore and I walked out onto the pitch. Terry came out and joined us and we stood together in a line watching the Arsenal players coming out.

The game exploded after five minutes when Gazza scored a fantastic free kick from thirty-five yards. David Seaman, the Arsenal goalkeeper, got nowhere near it. It was perfectly placed at the top corner and even today is considered one of the best free kicks seen at Wembley.

Gary Lineker as usual went and scored two more goals and we finished up worthy winners on the day in a 3–1 win. It really sunk in then that we were going back again to play in the Cup Final at Wembley.

The final had exactly the same atmosphere as the semi because of the high-profile reputation of the two managers, the legendary Brian Clough for Nottingham Forest, and Terry. I remember as the teams walked out onto the pitch Cloughie grabbed hold of Terry's hand and they walked out onto the pitch hand-in-hand. It was hilarious as Terry looked a bit embarrassed but Cloughie was enjoying himself. He may have had a little tipple before the game.

Gazza was psyched up and in the first few minutes he put in a hell of a tackle against Garry Parker. If the referee, Roger Milford, had booked Gazza for that it would have calmed him down, but instead he just gave him a lecture and the game continued. Gazza was thus still psyched up when he went into Gary Charles, the Nottingham Forest right back and, unfortunately for us and for him, Gazza suffered an injury to his knee. He tried to carry on playing but his cruciate ligament had gone and, after Stuart Pearce scored from the free kick that Gazza had given away, Gazza had to be carried off on a stretcher.

Paul Stewart equalised to take the game into extra time. The tension was mounting as we went on to the pitch to talk to the players as the extra time was about to start. Terry, Dougie and I were out there motivating the players and I was amazed that Brian Clough and his staff just sat on the bench, though Stuart Pearce and Des Walker of Nottingham Forest were trying to motivate their players. Even at that time I could see the managerial and coaching skills of Pearcie coming through. Both sides came close but we won a corner. Gary Mabbutt got his head to the ball. Unfortunately for Forest, Des Walker deflected the ball past Mark Crossley, the Nottingham Forest keeper, to give us the cup. The crowd went mad. The celebrations went on and I don't think we left the pitch for an hour.

Afterwards, Terry went off to do his press conference. I wandered over to the Nottingham Forest dressing room. Most of the players had gone to the VIP players' lounge. As I walked into that steamy Forest dressing room, Ronnie Fenton and Alan Hill, Cloughie's assistants, were sprawled across the benches. I know what it feels like to lose a cup final. I lost one with Epsom and Ewell in the FA Vase final and in our 1987 match versus Coventry when David Pleat was our manager when we had been odds-on favourites to win. So I was just consoling Ronnie and Alan when out of the shower room came Brian Clough, towel wrapped around him. He looked over to me and said, 'You come to take the piss, Edward?'

'No, Guvnor,' I said. 'I know what it's like to lose a final and was just commiserating with the lads.'

With that he walked over, grabbed me by the balls and said, 'Good lad. Now fuck off.'

Despite Cloughie's gripping farewell to me, we went back to the celebrations which went on until the early hours of the morning. A good time was had by everyone as we were now getting ready to go on tour to play two games in Japan, one playing the Japanese national side.

The problem was that we flew to Hawaii for a week's holiday before the game. With hindsight this was the wrong way round as we should have visited Hawaii on the way back. Although we had a couple of days light training in Hawaii, I don't think we were in the right state of mind to play in Japan a week after the Cup Final.

Part of the tour was based on Gary Lineker having a central role in the team to play against Japan, but Gary had been playing with the England squad and had sustained a foot injury, so he wasn't on top form to play against Japan. He was flying in to Tokyo from Malaysia as he had come direct from the England squad rather than via Hawaii with the rest of the team. He was about to sign a contract with a Japanese club, Grampus Eight, which was why they wanted to see him play against the Japanese national team.

Even before the game, there were problems. Mr Ito, one of the Japan Football Association officials, came to the hotel and greeted us and the players, telling us that we were going to see Mount Fuji and they would be holding a reception for us that night. We travelled to Mount Fuji on the amazing bullet train and the scenery was fantastic en route but, disappointingly, when we arrived there was a dense fog so we didn't actually get to see the volcano.

The Japanese laid on excellent food and drink on the train for the return journey and treated us very well. Mr Ito got us all together back at the hotel and then said they would like one of our officials to give a speech at the evening's reception. Everybody else 'volunteered' me to do it, so I asked Mr Ito what he expected me to say. He replied that he hoped I would say how much we liked Japan and how well they had looked after us.

With all the lads sitting around me, I thought I would be a bit cheeky so I started by saying to him, 'When I was in Malaya we captured a few of your people who had remained in Malaya after the Second World War.'

He responded saying in his strong accent: 'They deserters. No good.'

All the lads were now smiling. Then I said to him, 'Will it be alright if I mention at the reception in my welcoming speech the Bridge over the River Kwai.'

He got agitated and said, 'Oh no, no, no,' while waving his arms.

The lads were laughing and before he settled down I said '… or maybe Pearl Harbour'. He stormed off. Later he came back and said that they had decided after all not to have a speaker at the reception, so at least I got out of that.

As it turned out, we were hopeless in the game. The week in Hawaii had not done the players any good. We hardly had a kick through all ninety minutes and were beaten 4–1. Gary, feeling his injury, hardly touched the ball, much to the disappointment of the sell-out Japanese crowd. We missed Gazza, who hadn't toured with us as he was still suffering from his cruciate injury, and Terry, who hadn't come on the trip and had left Dougie Livermore, Ray Clemence and myself to look after the squad. If Terry had come with us maybe we would have been in better shape for the game. I assume Terry was not on the trip because he was involved in the negotiations with Alan Sugar to take over the club from Irving Scholar.

When we got back to England and the start of the new season, Alan Sugar was already in place as the new chairman of Tottenham, with Terry as chief executive. Where we had been used to Irving Scholar being actively involved in the club and coming down to chat to the players, even putting on charity events where he played a game or two, we saw very little of Alan Sugar. We never sat down with him or were introduced to him but his wife, Ann, and his children were often at the club and I got on well with them and got the occasional kiss on the cheek from Ann. I even bought an Amstrad video player from his son, Daniel. Alan Sugar himself remained somewhat aloof and removed from the day-to-day football activities and concentrated instead on the business side of the club, so I didn't see much of him.

There were a few occasions when we met. The first was when he and Ann and a couple of friends came into Scribes one night. They had been to an Italian restaurant, and when Alan called me over to the bar he said to me, 'Hey, Ted we've just had a meal at an Italian restaurant and the owner has told me that two of his waiters have played in Italy in the Italian league and we can sign them because they are free agents.'

For various reasons they wouldn't have been able to play for us unless they had enough international caps so I said, 'Are they internationals?'

'I don't know,' said Alan.

'Mr Chairman, if they're not internationals, they have no chance of getting work permits to play for us,' I said. 'What are they doing waiting on tables if they're good enough to be professional footballers in Italy?'

At that point Terry came over. I mentioned the conversation to him and Terry gave a sigh and said to Alan, 'You should leave the football to us.'

The only other occasion when I had a one-to-one conversation with Alan Sugar was when Yugoslavia was breaking up in April 1992. He was in his office at the club having a discussion with Terry, Jonathan Crystal, Tottenham's lawyer, and Eddie Ashby, the club's finance man, Ray Clemence and Dougie Livermore. After the meeting Sugar called me over and said, 'We might be able to get some good players out of this Yugoslav break up.' It was obvious that someone had informed him of the situation and he was right that there were some good players in the Balkans.

THE WAILING WALL

Terry's nightclub, Scribes, was a popular location and a lot of personalities used to come down – Jimmy Tarbuck, Phil Collins, George Shearing, Barbara Windsor, Britt Ekland, to name but a few. Britt Ekland had a meal with us one night and told us about her six-year-old son who loved football. I remember telling her to give him a few years and then I would come and have a look at him to see if he was any good.

We had some great times at Scribes and one of the biggest laughs was when George Shearing, the blind pianist, was invited by Eric Hall, one of the big musical agents, to come and perform at the club. When Terry and I arrived, Eric told us that George would be appearing. We thought he was kidding because George had just finished a UK-wide tour. The entertainment didn't start till about 11 at night when Eric got up and announced that George was there.

To our surprise, in walked George with his white stick and a lady guiding him. Eric introduced him and he sat down at the piano. Dennis, the regular pianist, was thrilled to let George have his seat. After an excellent performance of about forty-five minutes, George got up and thanked everybody to rapturous applause. Off he went to the car waiting outside to take him away. Terry said to Eric, 'How the hell did you get him to come down here?'

Eric, who was a great joker and a laugh a minute, said, 'Oh I told him a little lie. I told him this was a private party at the London Palladium.'

Another time I was in Scribes when the infamous gangster 'Mad' Frankie Fraser came in with a young lady who he clearly wanted to impress. His father-in-law, Tommy Wisbey, one of the Great Train Robbers, was already there with his wife. Terry wasn't keen having any of them in the club but he wasn't there that night.

I had met Frankie on a previous occasion when he had heard me sing so he came over and said he would like me to sing a song for his friend. I wasn't in the mood so I tried to put him off by saying, 'Not now, Frankie, maybe later.'

'Now,' he said slowly and forcefully, 'we'll be going soon.' You didn't argue with Frankie so I sang *Fly Me To The Moon*, which was where I would have preferred to be. He left the club happy and I was happy that he left.

The cracks in the relationship between Terry and Alan Sugar were coming to the fore. There was clearly a clash of personalities between them, which resulted in Sugar sacking Terry in 1993. There followed a well-publicised court case when Terry secured a temporary reinstatement. The players were devastated that Terry was going, as were the fans, who demonstrated strongly outside the ground and apparently even went to Sugar's house to protest.

As Terry and I drove out of the ground, there were crowds of people blocking White Hart Lane, cheering Terry, banging on the cars in support and shouting 'Sugar out! Sugar out!' The police were there in significant numbers trying to control the crowd and prevent them getting in. I wasn't surprised at the level of support Terry had from the fans but was amazed by the number who felt so strongly that they came out to protest.

After Terry left Tottenham, I suspected that my days there were numbered, although one of the directors confirmed that whatever happened I would be paid up to the end of my contract. I flew out to my old stomping ground at Tampa for a holiday and when I returned, as previously mentioned, Ossie was given the task of delivering the *coup de grâce*. So I was working for my last few weeks at Tottenham and was involved in a legal action with Sugar over the early termination of my roll-on contract.

I was quite confident that I would get offers from other clubs but in the meantime we got wind of Terry being in the running for the England job after Graham Taylor had got the sack. I knew that Jimmy Armfield, the England captain in the 1960s, was advising the FA on the next manager of England and I know he was very keen on Terry taking the job. So I was both disappointed about leaving Tottenham and anticipating what the future might hold.

Terry in the meantime had phoned me a few times and asked me if I fancied a trip to Israel to look at the Russian team St Petersburg that was over there. A former Blackburn director and chairman, Walter Hubert, was looking to take over or buy into the team. Terry was due to go but because of the England situation, he wasn't able to make it so he asked me to stand in. Everything was paid for with a £1000 fee so I agreed to go.

I spoke to Walter Hubert's associate who promised me that I would have a four-star hotel, would be met at the airport and would be driven around to various places in Tel Aviv to watch the players and give my opinion. When I arrived in Tel Aviv I was met, as arranged, by the driver. When I asked him the name of the hotel, he said, 'It's not very far,' so I wasn't given the name until we drove into some farmland and I found I would be staying at a kibbutz.

I wasn't too happy because I knew Terry wouldn't have accepted that and I suspected the business man had cut costs when he knew I would be coming instead. I managed to phone him and he assured me that they would look after me, even though the normal routine in a kibbutz was that everyone helped each other. I had my own little apartment in the commune and the couple who seemed to be my main contacts along with their twenty-something daughter looked after me.

They brought me food and bowls of fruit and generally tended to me so after the initial surprise I settled down and felt quite at home. They used to have entertainment such as music and dancing in the evening and their daughter drove me around to a couple of training grounds where the St Petersburg players were training. I made a full assessment of all the players and after watching one game against Maccabi, one of the top Israeli teams, I made up my mind and wrote a report for Walter Hubert.

I then had a few days to myself. The couple showed me around Israel and Jerusalem as a tourist, including where Jesus was supposed to have been born and where he was crucified. I found it a fascinating place with all the markets, full of bustle and activity, noise and animals and people dressed in Middle Eastern clothing – it was like being in the old Bob Hope and Bing Crosby film *Road To Morocco*.

I hadn't heard anything from Terry about the England job so I was beginning to doubt that it would come off. Two days before I was due to fly home, the couple asked me if I would like to see the Wailing Wall. Although I had heard of it, I didn't know much about it. When we arrived I walked into this huge square. It was an amazing sight with an enormous ancient wall that looked about 100 feet high to me, with people all along the wall with their heads against the wall wailing and praying.

When I asked the couple to explain what it was all about, the wife said, 'If you write a wish down on a piece of paper and stick it in a slot between the bricks in the wall, lean your forehead against the wall and pray for it to happen, your wish may be granted. It does happen.'

I wrote on my piece of paper, 'I want a job with Terry and England' and reached up as high as I could in the wall, standing on my tiptoes, and slotted it between the ancient bricks. It was a strange sensation as I did it because I felt a sense of warmth and peace. It was a stunning place and I shall never forget it.

Back in the kibbutz on my last night in Israel, they had put on some entertainment. I received a call from Terry saying that he was having a second interview for the England job but nothing was definite because there were still a few obstacles to be sorted out. He was surprised that I was enjoying the kibbutz so much. I made him laugh as I said, 'This could do me. I might join Maccabi football club.'

'Shalom' – Hebrew for 'Peace go with you' – he shouted. We both had a good laugh.

When I arrived back in England, I sent all the reports off to Walter Hubert and he was satisfied with that. I forgave him for not putting me in a four-star hotel, because secretly I was happy in the kibbutz, but I didn't tell him that because I was hoping he would pay me some more money. He didn't.

Terry was still hesitating about taking the job because he was still not happy with a couple of things. I didn't know whether it was politics or real contractual issues and it looked at one point as though it wasn't going to happen. I was starting to feel a bit down and, contemplating an uncertain future, I went and had a drink with Terry at Scribes, when he told me that some members of the FA governing body were reluctant for him to bring in his own staff. He had already requested that Dave Sexton and Don Howe should join him but they were both on a part-time basis. With me it would be even more complicated because I would be full-time. I reconciled myself to the fact that it probably wasn't going to happen.

About a week later, Terry called me unexpectedly and said, 'It's all been sorted.' I was all ears. He continued, 'Don and Dave are already on board together with Dave Butler, all on a part-time basis.' He didn't mention me, making me think that he was about to deliver bad news. There was a bit of a gap in the conversation when he seemed to sense my disappointment and then he said, 'Right, you start at the FA at Lancaster Gate eight o'clock Monday morning. I'll see you there.'

That was typical Terry to make me wait for the good news. I didn't even ask him what the money was, what the contract was, even what the precise job was – the sense of exhilaration was overwhelming. All I knew was that I was about to work with the England national team – my dream job. Not bad for a butcher from South London.

I drove home that night on cloud nine. I phoned my sons as soon as I got in (we didn't have mobiles in those days), then my ex-wife, my sister and brother-in-law – all the important people in my life. As I went to bed that night I remembered the Wailing Wall and said a quiet 'Thank you'. Now I realise that sometimes miracles do happen.

Later I had a good laugh with Terry when he related that when he had told the FA that he wanted to bring in Dave Sexton and me, they had said, 'They're a bit old aren't they?' to which Terry had retorted, 'I want them on my staff, I'm not wanting them to fucking play.'

ENGLAND, MY ENGLAND

On Monday morning on my arrival in Lancaster Gate I was met by David Bloomfield, who showed me up to my new office. There were ribbons around the desk and a notice saying 'Welcome, Ted, to the FA,' which I thought was a nice touch. I immediately felt at home.

I was then told that my new title would be assistant to the manager and chief scout. It was getting better and better as this was a completely new role in the FA and I had assumed that I would simply be chief scout. Being told that I was appointed as assistant to Terry was an amazing feeling. David put a box of business cards on my desk showing my new title. I was overjoyed and just wished my mum and dad and my brother, Alf, had still been alive because they would have been so proud of me.

Our first few months with England were spent building up the national squad, taking over from the previous manager, Graham Taylor. It was amazing that we had no reports left behind on the players so I assume Graham had taken everything on the team with him when he left. We started from scratch, which was not necessarily a bad approach as it gave us an opportunity to kick off with a clean sheet.

Terry said we must have a rundown on every player in the leagues, going right back to their grandparents, to see if they were eligible to play for England. He mentioned a specific incident during our time at Tottenham. Maurice Setters, Jack Charlton's number two for the Republic of Ireland team, had phoned me to say that he had picked a young boy called Chris Kinnear, a first year pro at Tottenham, to play for the Republic against Spain's under-18 side in a forthcoming tournament.

Maurice said all the paperwork would be sent through to us and I was to tell the boy that he had been selected. When Terry came in he said that was great news and told me to call the boy up. He came into the office; I congratulated him and he said, 'What for?'

I told him he had been picked for Eire's under-18 side.

He said, 'Where's Eire?'

I said, 'It's the Republic of Ireland and Jack Charlton's the manager.'

'I know that but where's Eire?' he asked.

'That's Ireland,' I said. 'You must have Irish blood if you've been picked for Ireland.'

'I didn't know that,' he said.

'Is your mum or dad Irish?' I asked.

He said they weren't.

I said, 'It must be your grandparents,' but he said he didn't know. This was getting comical so Terry told him to go away and find out his family history. About two days later he came back and knocked on my office door before training started. I was on my own.

He said, 'My mum's gone back to the 1800s and we can't find any Irish heritage.'

'Are you sure?' I asked.

'Absolutely certain.'

So I phoned Maurice Setters and asked him, 'Maurice, how did you pick this boy because he's been back to the 1800s and he has no Irish in him?'

I heard him say to Jack Charlton, who must have been sitting beside him, 'The boy Kinnear's not Irish.'

I asked Maurice again, 'How did you come to the conclusion that he was Irish?'

'With a name like Kinnear he must be,' said Maurice.

I told him he must have been thinking of Joe Kinnear, the Irish Republic international who had played for Tottenham but who was now in management at Wimbledon. So Terry called the boy in and said, 'Don't worry about Ireland. Maybe you'll play for England instead.'

As he walked out of the door, I called to him and said, 'Chris, you're absolutely sure your grandmother didn't have it off with an Irish milkman because that would qualify you.'

Terry said, 'Behave yourself,' but the lad smiled and got back to his training.

As I mentioned earlier, now we were at England, Terry wanted us to get a full history of each potential player. I got the secretaries at the club to contact every club in the country to get every player's background and parentage down to their grandparents and great-grandparents to make sure they would qualify to play for England because we didn't want another Chris Kinnear incident.

During training sessions, Terry would sometimes get me to play a match official so that he could see how players would react to dodgy refereeing decisions. As they were playing I would have to let a couple of iffy off sides go or would signal a free kick in scoreable positions. This would generate a rush of blood to the likes of Stuart Pearce and Tony Adams, who would let me know what they thought in no uncertain terms. Terry would step in to let them know that if they behaved like that in a game they would be carded and that they had to learn how to accept difficult decisions. These sessions always generated a lot of banter but ended with smiles all round.

David Davies, the Executive Director of the FA, invited me to join him to see Crystal Palace versus Manchester United at the former's ground, which turned out to be an infamous game. I was already planning to go because I was interested in seeing the potential of the players on both teams. David Davies was a keen Manchester United fan and he wasn't too enthusiastic about driving to Crystal Palace because it is a difficult ground to find if you're not familiar with that side of the river. But I was from South London so I was happy to drive us there.

We arrived quite early and had a pleasant time talking to Alex Ferguson, Bobby Charlton and a few other dignitaries. It was a lively game with good football from both sides. Manchester United took the lead before Southgate equalised for Crystal Palace, which pleased me because we had taken him into the squad. He was playing well and I knew that a number of people in the game hadn't been too sure about him for England.

Cantona then got into trouble and after his second booking he was sent off. David Davies and I were in the directors' box, which is close to one side of the tunnel in the corner of the pitch. Cantona was clearly upset at being sent off and was in any case already agitated so David Davies and I could sense that trouble was coming.

The Crystal Palace crowd was going mad. The atmosphere was electric and the air was blue with threats against Cantona. As he walked past the directors' box, a fan came storming down the stairs from the terracing towards Cantona, screaming racial abuse. Before the stewards and players could usher Cantona into the tunnel, he saw the fan coming towards him and suddenly leapt over the barrier and kung fu kicked the fan in the chest. The man went down like a sack of logs.

Now everyone was jumping on Cantona and marshalling him into the tunnel. The game ended in a 1–1 draw and after the incident David Davies said he would have to stay behind to deal with the press so I left as he didn't want me hanging around. Having heard the racial abuse he had to endure that day, I can understand how Cantona reacted as he did. Nowadays such racial abuse would not be tolerated.

In 1994, I moved to Harefield. I had bought a small terraced house in a new development which was built on a piece of land that had formerly been used in an episode where they filmed the TV series *Inspector Morse* with John Thaw. When the garden was finished, I decided to have a pond put in and equipped it with a filter before filling it with koi carp. I enjoyed watching the fish until one morning I went to feed them and saw a snake swimming around and diving into the reeds. I wasn't having this. As I lay down on the grass beside the pond, watching and waiting silently, my jungle instincts kicked in.

After about fifteen minutes it came up for air. I grabbed it by the neck and hauled it out. It was about two-feet long and was writhing in my hands as I flung it over the hedge into the field behind my house. The field was full of cows so I thought they would sort it out.

About a week later, it happened again. I don't know if it was the same snake but this time it had got hold of a frog, which was lodged in its jaws. Yet again I lay in wait for it. Sure enough, up it came, still with the poor frog in its mouth, as I grabbed it and popped it into a plastic bag. Throwing it into the field hadn't worked the first time so I decided to take it along to the pet shop in the village.

As I walked in carrying my writhing plastic bag, I asked the lady who ran the shop with her daughter if she wanted it and I put the bag on the counter. As I opened it, both women screamed in unison. They clearly didn't want it, so I walked home with the bag, and the snake and the frog were thrown into the field again.

Although my first encounter with the pet-shop owners may not have endeared me to my new neighbours, I did better with my next encounter. It was with a very attractive lady who jointly ran a shop in the village with her partner. I bought a shovel from Caroline but when it turned out to be faulty I took it back and we started to chat. When I told her that I was new to the village, she filled me in on all the local gossip. About a year later she and her partner split up and Caroline and I then got together and were a couple for over ten years. I was probably not the best of partners but we had many happy times together and, now that she is in a new relationship, we're still friends.

I found a good curry house called the Royal Gurkha, owned by ex-Gurkhas, not far from Harefield Hospital and would pop in for a curry and a bottle of wine. One quiet evening I was sitting on my own at my usual table, when a tall, elegant woman came in with a smart-looking Asian man. He shook hands with the owner and then they walked to their table, which was situated in a quiet alcove.

To my amazement, it turned out to be Princess Diana in a dark wig. I asked the owner if it was really the princess and he assured me that it was. 'They come in from time to time and always have the same table,' he said and from then on he always gave me that table. I was more convinced than ever that Harefield was turning out to be a great place to live.

The best period for me with the England squad was during the 1994–96 period, qualifying for the European Cup, along with a lot of friendly matches that we played against other national teams, such as Nigeria and Japan.

Before the tournament started, we had arranged games in Hong Kong and China for a pre-tournament warm-up. It was suggested that I go out to China to suss out the hotels and the Beijing Workers' Stadium, the city's main stadium. Reports had it that the pitch wasn't in good condition and a year previously, David Seaman, our goalkeeper, had damaged his ankle playing for Arsenal in the same stadium.

So Terry suggested to Graham Kelly and David Davies at the FA that I should go out and sort everything out in advance. David thought it was a great idea so I flew out to China. There were three games in the stadium over the Saturday and Sunday when I arrived. You can imagine after two days of games what the pitch was like and the mess around the stadium was appalling.

I was assured after the games that everything would be cleaned up and the pitch would be ready by the Monday.

When I arrived at the stadium at lunchtime on the Monday, it was still in the same state, pitch- and rubbish-wise. I called a meeting with the stadium officials and through the interpreter said, 'You promised me that this would all be cleaned up. Where are your head groundsman and your ground staff?' I was told it was their day off.

'Right, if this place is not cleaned up by tomorrow morning and the pitch sorted out, we'll call the tournament off,' I said. There was a bit of a panic and while I was still there the groundsman rode up on his bike. Through the interpreter I said, 'Tell him to get off his fat arse and get the place ready by tomorrow.'

I got up early the next morning and was driven to the stadium. There must have been 150 workers on the pitch and around the stadium. By lunchtime that day it had started to look better but I still didn't let them think that I was satisfied. Over the next two days I attended two or three press conferences in which the Chinese press called me 'Mr Ted' and I started to build a decent rapport with them. Two members of the press spoke perfect English and it was they who gave me my nickname. The team was due to fly out to China on the Thursday and I had spoken at length to Terry, assuring him that everything was fine. The stadium was OK and the hotels were fine so the tournament went ahead.

When the team arrived at Beijing airport on the Thursday and walked off the plane into the terminal, the press were waiting and a couple of thousand Chinese spectators were looking on. As I walked forward to greet Terry and David, the crowd started clapping and shouting 'Mr Ted. Mr Ted.'

'What's going on here?' asked Terry.

'They love me here,' I said.

Terry laughed. He recognised this as a quote from Jimmy Hill from an incident involving him and Des Lynam when they were at a Merseyside derby between Liverpool and Everton. Terry and Jimmy were there to comment on the game with Des as the presenter. Some reconstruction was being done to the stadium at that time so, unusually, they had to walk around the entire side of the pitch to get to the gantry where the interviews were to take place.

Terry and Des were not too happy having to walk such a length in front of 40 000 people but Jimmy strode a few yards ahead of them. The crowd spontaneously erupted into a chant of 'Jimmy Hill's a wanker,' to which Jimmy, who looked and sounded like Bruce Forsyth, turned to Terry and Des and said confidently in his distinctive voice, 'They love me here.' Terry said it had been hilarious at the time.

After we left China we flew into Hong Kong to play an informal group called the Hong Kong Eleven, made up of old professionals from England and Europe with a few Chinese players added in. It was a friendly affair all round. The lads were pleased that we were at the end of the tour and were looking forward to returning home in a couple of days. During the stay in Hong Kong, it was coming up to Gazza's birthday so it was arranged that we would have a party in a private room at a nightclub.

All the players were looking forward to a night out away from the public eye. Terry didn't want to go and I certainly didn't want to go so he asked Bryan Robson, the former midfield legend from Manchester United who was then on our coaching staff, to look after the squad. I think Terry misjudged the situation by allowing Bryan to take charge, seeing as Bryan still thought of himself as a player and one of the boys. He really hadn't acknowledged to himself that he was now on the management side and needed to keep the lads in order.

As the night wore on, some members of the public managed to get into the private room and the players were starting to get the worse for wear but still no real harm was being done. They were just enjoying their night with their usual high spirits. They were celebrating Gazza's birthday but photos were taken of Gazza lying back in a reclining high-backed armchair that the press subsequently dubbed as a 'dentist's chair' with the lads one-by-one pouring champagne into his mouth.

Some of the players had been wearing expensive designer shirts and the next day pictures appeared in the press of Teddy Sheringham and Steve McManaman with their shirts torn, drinking and roaring with laughter. The press had a field day implying that the team were all drunk and incapable and criticising their behaviour as being inappropriate for the England team with a big tournament coming up. All it really was, was just a boys' night out celebrating Gazza's birthday. When the story broke, Terry was livid that these things were allowed to get out of hand on a night that should have been a private event, but that was not the end of it because a further incident occurred on the flight home.

Terry had decided that the players could sit together in the upper cabin on the plane and that the staff and FA councillors would be downstairs in the main cabin. Some of the FA members had wanted to go upstairs and leave the players downstairs but Terry stood by his decision. It was a night flight and several hours in, when everyone was dozing, one of the air stewardesses came down and whispered to Terry, who was sitting next to me, that there was a problem upstairs with the players.

The FA councillors overheard this and wanted to know what was going on, so Terry said to me, 'Ted, go and sort it out. See what you can do.'

I climbed up the stairs to the top deck. I heard a bit of shouting and as my head popped up onto the upper deck, a lot of the players started chanting and clapping, 'There's only one Teddy Buxton.'

'Behave yourselves,' I told them. 'What's the problem?'

I then saw a passenger who was the worse for wear staggering about, who we later found out was an airline pilot with Cathay

Pacific who was flying to London to pick up a plane and fly it back to Hong Kong. One of the players said that this passenger had been a bloody nuisance and that he had been climbing all over the place and one of the players had pushed him back into his seat. In doing so, a TV screen had been damaged. But everything settled down and I returned to my seat. The rest of the flight was uneventful.

But the story broke in the press the next day when we were back in London with claims that the players had run riot on the plane. This was of course tacked on to the exaggerated tales about the dentist's chair. Cathay Pacific had apparently complained to the FA about the broken TV screen and there was speculation in the media that it had been Gazza who had caused the damage. I am certain that Gazza wasn't responsible for the damage because he hated flying and tended to prefer to sleep during a flight. I suspected the real culprit had been the drunken passenger.

Terry called a meeting of players and staff to settle the matter and pointed out that if the truth were to come out the airline pilot would probably lose his job, so it was unanimously agreed between everyone, players and staff, that we would all chip in to pay for the damage and would accept collective responsibility. Cathay Pacific accepted the apology and payment but the story did not go away and was still surfacing in the press when we started training for the competition at Bisham Abbey.

During a break in training when we needed to get some fluids back in the players' systems, I handed a bottle of power drink to Robbie Fowler. Being a bit of a comedian, Robbie dropped his head back to mirror the incident in the 'dentist's chair' and I poured the drink into his mouth. Next day the papers were full of pictures of me and Robbie with headlines joking about footballers' behaviour. I still have the photograph in pride of place at home.

ASTON VILLA

We had a problem with our centre halves when Tony Adams and Gary Pallister were injured at the same time. 'We need another backup player,' said Terry and I suggested Stevie Bruce, who was a player that I knew very well and who everyone thought was the best uncapped player in England at the time. He had just arrived at Birmingham on a free transfer from Manchester United.

'How old must he be now?' asked Terry.

'Probably in his early thirties,' I said. 'He's still playing well and Leslie Compton wasn't capped for England until he was about thirty-four in the late 1950s.'

'Good shout,' said Terry. 'Phone him up and see if he would fancy it.'

I had known from the past that Stevie would play through pain. He had been a player with me at Gillingham before he went onto big things with Norwich and Manchester United, and on one occasion he even tried to play with a broken leg against Newport County. I phoned Stevie and he said, 'Oh, Ted. I'm injured.'

I couldn't believe it. I think he had a groin tear or something along those lines and this would probably have been his one chance to get an England cap to round off his great career. Unfortunately, age was against him and he didn't heal as fast as he would have done when younger, so he didn't get to play for his country. So with Stevie unable to play, we brought in Colin Cooper from Middlesbrough, who was a versatile player able to play right back or centre half as did Gareth Southgate, who was always in the squad after that. We also brought in Ugochuku Ehiogu from Aston Villa.

We then had a sponsored game against the Japanese at Wembley. It was quite useful for Terry to have these friendly games so that he could assess the players he would select for his final squad. Because we would be going on to Hong Kong and China, it was essential that Terry had a good look at our players beforehand. Terry was popular with the crowd and Wembley was packed out, with everyone having high expectations of what he could achieve with the team. There was a sense of anticipation in the country at the time and it was a good game against Japan, with England winning 2–1.

After the game, the players got a commemorative medal from the Japanese. As the players went up the Wembley stairs to collect their medals from the Japanese officials, the staff were waiting, below and Morris Keston, by now a great pal of Terry's and mine, turned to me and said, 'Do you know what, Ted, I think the Japanese were more wicked than the Germans during the war.'

'You're probably right, Morris, but looking at that lot, they're too young, except that one at the end,' I replied. 'He looks like a Japanese general to me. He looks as if he could have lopped off a few heads in Singapore.'

'Hey, you'll be in trouble if you start saying things like that in front of them,' a bystander warned, but there were a few smiles all round.

The reception after the game was a hilarious affair as far as I was concerned. Terry, George Graham, Lawrie McMenemy, a few FA councillors and I were all on one table. The Japanese contingent was to be introduced to us, so as they came past our table in a line, we all stood up. Obviously, Terry was the first to greet them, together with the representatives of the FA. When they came towards us, I turned round to our guys and said, 'Don't forget to bow to them to show respect. When you bow, they bow too, so make sure you keep bowing to them.'

When they came to me, I not only bowed the first time but I kept bowing and of course the Japanese kept bowing too. This went on until the very last man arrived, the one I had previously described as the Japanese general. He gripped my hand and I bowed while everyone else looked on in quiet anticipation because Terry had previously told me to behave myself.

I bowed three times and he bowed three times. Not knowing how well he spoke English, I said slowly and distinctly, 'Did you enjoy the game?'

He bowed again and said, 'Ah, yes, very much,' with a very pronounced Japanese accent.

I said, 'Ah, good,' but then I got carried away and added, 'but not as much as Pearl Harbour.'

There was a deathly silence, apart from a sharp intake of breath by Terry who nudged me sharply and whispered, 'Behave yourself.'

But then the Japanese man threw back his head and roared with laughter and said, 'Very good, very good,' and was still laughing as they all went on to their tables.

I got some sharp looks from the England dignitaries and I think it was Lawrie McMenemy who said, 'You took a chance there. It's a good job he had a sense of humour.'

After the meal as the Japanese contingent was leaving, the Japanese man looked over across the room at me, smiling and waving his arms at me and shouting out, 'Good luck'. Then he left the line, walked over and shook my hand again, bowing as he did so. Of course I bowed back, several times. He was still smiling as he left, so an international incident had been narrowly avoided, much to the relief of the FA.

When we got to the actual matches to get through to the European Cup, we didn't start off too well against Switzerland. We struggled a bit to get the 1–1 draw to qualify for the next round.

We had a scouting system which involved everyone. Before the tournament Bryan Robson, Mike Ferguson, Kenny Brown, George

Boardman, Mick Kelly, Don Howe, Dave Sexton, others on the staff and me would go out to games to assess prospective members of the squad playing for their own clubs. Those possibles would then be invited to the training ground at Bisham Abbey to train with Terry and the rest of the coaching staff and, once we knew the group we would be playing in, we would then fly to various venues around Europe to assess the opposition players, how their teams were set up and the various systems that they played.

We, the assessors, would prepare reports on all of the games and players we had reviewed and these would go to Terry. Terry, Bryan, Don, Mike and I would sit for hours discussing players and tactics while Terry listened to everybody's opinion. Before he finalised the choice of players to make up the final squad, he would have the forty prospective players come in for training.

Terry would also bring in the young under-21 players, including, for example, the Neville brothers, Gary and Phil, Robbie Fowler, Ray Parlour and many other potential youngsters and would play them to get them used to the atmosphere of an England camp. There were always people inside the clubs, such as the chairmen of the league clubs, ringing me or taking me aside to the directors' lounge at games at their clubs, to recommend certain players in their own team.

One great example of this was Doug Ellis, who owned Aston Villa and tended to act as if he ran the entire club as manager, coach and everything else as well. Doug was a real character in the football world. Terry named him Sergeant Bilko after the Phil Silver's television show because he always had some enterprising project on the go. Looking back, I think it was a great time for him. He was always recommending his players. Ugo Ehiogu didn't make the final squad but we decided to bring in Gareth Southgate because of his versatility.

After we brought Gareth into the squad I was often a visitor to Villa Park to keep an eye on him and the other players. Terry came with me on one occasion, and when we drove into Villa Park we found the roads had been closed. 'What are we going to do now?' asked Terry.

So I drove on to the closed road, where an official and a security man came over. I rolled down the window and said, 'We've got to get through – I've got Terry Venables, the England manager here.'

The security man stood back and saluted me and said, 'OK Mr Croker.'

He mistook me for Ted Croker who was the Secretary at the FA and I must have looked rather like him because other people had made the same mistake. With that the barriers went up and we were allowed in. Terry roared with laughter and said, 'How did we get away with that?'

'They're always mistaking me for Ted Croker. At least they got half my name right.'

On another occasion Doug Ellis decided to come to Scribes, Terry's nightclub, with a couple of his friends and with a lady on his arm. We had a nice meal together and the karaoke started around 11.30 p.m. involving a group of us including Eric Hall, Terry's agent at the time. I sang the first couple of songs, ending with a duet with Nancy, Terry's daughter, who had a good voice, belting out *Up Where We Belong* from *An Officer and a Gentleman*.

Doug came over to me and said, 'My lady would like to do a song.' In his Bilko voice, he added, 'Well she is an opera singer.'

I told him we didn't have any opera but perhaps a Sinatra song would go down well so I chose *All The Way*. Although she had a nice voice, it wasn't exactly Sinatra, but halfway through the song Doug suddenly got up on stage, put his arm around her and started singing with her. To be honest he didn't have a good singing voice but it went down a treat with the punters and I think Doug was quite chuffed the way things turned out.

My next visit to Villa Park came just after we had announced that Gareth Southgate had made the final squad together with

Stevie Stone, also from Aston Villa. At the time a few coaches and managers were a bit surprised when we put Stevie in the squad because they thought he was a good club player but were not convinced that he was of a calibre to play for England. But he proved everybody wrong. He did a great job for us in his time with the England squad. He was a workaholic and seemed to have three lungs as he could run and work all day.

I drew into the VIP car park and who drove alongside me in his Rolls Royce but Doug Ellis. He rolled down his window and I saw that with him he had a good looking young woman wearing a sash showing she had just won a beauty queen competition. Doug called, 'Did I ever tell you, Ted, that I played for Sheffield Wednesday?'

'I didn't know that, Chairman,' I said, taking the mickey. 'I wish I had seen you play. You would probably have been picked for the England squad.'

He guffawed good-humouredly. 'I don't know about that. This young lady has won a beauty contest.' I nodded an acknowledgement to the young lady and Doug invited me to come up to the boardroom.

Before I got there, he pulled me to one side and said, 'Come and see the lads in the dressing room.'

This was not a good time as the manager has his work cut out to prepare the team for the game and it was due to start within the hour. I told him to leave it but he could not be dissuaded, so we went in.

The first thing I saw was Gareth Southgate on a table having his ankle strapped. Doug bellowed, 'I told you I'd get you into the England team.'

There was a deathly silence and finally Gareth muttered something like, 'Hallo, Ted, are you OK?'

At that point, Brian Little, the team manager walked in and looked over at me and Doug.

I put my hands up and mouthed to him, 'Sorry.'

'No problems, Ted,' he replied, leading me to surmise that he was used to his chairman's interference and had grown used to coping with it.

We went up to the boardroom. Doug showed me into a separate room, an inner sanctum, where only the chairman and a couple of directors would gather. He poured me a glass of wine and said to the directors, 'This man's not only a talent spotter but he can sing a bit himself.'

'Not as well as you, Chairman,' I said.

With that there were a couple of embarrassed splutters and we moved on quickly to another subject. He is no longer actively involved in Aston Villa but his presence is still felt in the club and whenever we meet, we always have a nice chat. He always asks how Terry is – and I suspect there was a time when he would have liked Terry to take the manager's job at Villa.

FOOTBALL'S COMING HOME

In 1996 during the European cup, Gazza came to me one afternoon after training and said that he had left his favourite boots back in Newcastle. I asked if the kitman could arrange for someone to collect them and have them delivered to the training ground but Gazza was insistent that he had told two or three of his mates to fly down with the boots and he would pay for their plane fares. I had my suspicions about his real intentions so I went to have a chat with Terry.

We both came to the conclusion that Gazza wanted a few Geordie mates around him before the Scotland game so Terry said they could come down but Gazza had to put them up in a hotel some miles away and they were not to hang around the training ground. Gazza insisted that he would sort it out and there would be no trouble. As far as we knew, his mates flew down with the boots ready for the game against Scotland.

The stadium was a sell-out and the atmosphere was tense given the rivalry between England and Scotland. Half the crowd were Scotland supporters. The press had tended to favour Scotland because we hadn't been playing very well at that point, so the Scots were geared up for a victory.

We didn't do well in the first half but ten minutes into the second half a build up between Gareth Southgate and Gary Neville put us in the lead with a great header by Alan Shearer. Gordon Durie, Scotland's centre forward, drove into the box but was brought down by Tony Adams. Scotland was then awarded a penalty that could have brought them level but for David Seaman's great reaction save. The papers reported that he merely deflected Gary McAllister's ball with his elbow, but in my opinion he made a fantastic save.

The highlight of the game was our second goal, when Gazza made one of the best goals seen at Wembley. He took a pass from Darren Anderton, ran at the Scottish defence behind their midfield, went one-on-one against Colin Hendry, flicked it over Hendry's head with his left foot, went past Hendry as if he wasn't there and smashed the ball into the net past Andy Goram, the Scottish keeper. The whole stadium erupted and I think even the Scottish supporters appreciated the brilliance of Gazza's goal.

Scotland played well but David Seaman made a couple of good saves, including Gordon Durie's header. Seaman handled all the balls that Scotland were putting into his box but it was Gazza's show, although the subsequent celebrations were linked in the press with reference to the dentist's chair incident in China. Maybe having his favourite boots made all the difference to Gazza's game or perhaps it was simply having his Geordie mates with him that inspired him. Whatever the reason, it was certainly worth the air fares.

The game ended 2–0 and expectations for the next game versus Holland were very high, not least because Holland was considered one of the best sides in the tournament with a team full of world-class players.

On the morning of the match, with the police escorting us from Bisham Abbey to Wembley, the crowds on the streets, there from the early morning, were something I hadn't experienced since VE Day. Sitting on that coach and driving past all the people on the streets, some on their knees bowing to us, was an amazing experience and I could feel the sense of expectation of the whole squad as we drove to Wembley.

It was a ritual now that ten minutes before we arrived at Wembley Gazza would shout, 'Put the tape on,' and the coach driver would play *Football's Coming Home* by David Baddiel and Frank Skinner. On this occasion the driver put the tape on but it wouldn't play. Now the whole coach was panicking as the ritual was being broken, which could have been a bad omen. There is always a lot of superstition around the game and there seemed no alternative but to stop the coach to get the tape working.

Both of the police motorcycle escorts couldn't work out what was happening when the coach stopped. The front escort dropped back and spoke to the driver and the crowds now pressed forward from the pavement to the coach. The police were starting to get a bit anxious. The coach driver and Gazza were working on the tape and, miracle of miracles, it started up. I know what would have been the outcome if they hadn't got it going but once it started I could feel the rush of adrenaline running through the players.

We got into the Wembley dressing rooms and Terry started calming everyone down. As we were preparing for the game, Frank de Boer from the Dutch team arrived at our dressing room door and caught my eye. I went over to him and he asked me very politely if I would be able to get the signatures of all of our players on a Dutch pennant that he was holding in his hand. I was happy to help and said this was not a problem and told him to come and collect it after the game. It was an interesting pennant decorated in orange and grey so I went around everyone in the dressing room and all the staff and players signed it.

Meanwhile, Terry was again running through the playing system with the team. The other members of the coaching staff were going round talking to players. The defence and attacking set plays were put up on the wall with players digesting what was up there. The players went out to warm up. Mike Kelly was working the goalkeepers. Don Howe and Bryan Robson were warming up the outfield players. Terry and I were walking around talking to individuals. After all the warm-ups we all went back into the dressing room. The referees had been handed the team sheets. All the preliminaries had been done and the players who wanted to be strapped up and those who wanted their legs to be massaged were with Dave Butler and Alan Smith, the two physios.

When all this was underway, Terry said to me, 'Let's go and get some fresh air away from the smell of the liniment.'

We were standing outside in the tunnel opposite the Dutch dressing room when Clarence Seedorf, one of the Dutch players, came out with one of their coaches. It looked as though he was trying out a pair of boots as he was fully kitted out except that he was wearing a training bib and he was juggling the ball. When the coach mishandled the ball and it landed in my hands, I looked at them both and Seedorf said 'Thank you' to me.

I turned to Terry and said, 'I don't think they fancy this today.' With that I threw the ball up in the air and headed it back to Seedorf. He took it on his chest, nearly slipped; took the ball and they both went back into the dressing room.

'Behave yourself. You'll get them wound up,' said Terry.

'No, they have no chance,' I said. We walked back into our dressing room. I mentioned this to Alan Shearer and said, 'Alan, these Dutchmen are here for the taking.'

'You're not wrong,' he replied.

When the two teams walked out on that Wembley pitch, the noise was absolutely deafening. I don't think I had experienced anything quite like it before.

The Holland game was described by most people in the media as being one of the most spectacular England performances ever. We outplayed the Dutch side in every department. Our pass and movement play was absolutely brilliant. Our running off the ball completely flummoxed the Dutch side. When players like Bergkamp, De Boer and Seedorf were on the ball, the way we closed them down was exactly the way Terry had planned the game and the response from our players was 100 per cent.

We were 4–0 up and didn't realise at the time that if the score had stayed that way Scotland would also have qualified to go on to the next stage but when Holland scored near the end of the game, it put Scotland out of the competition. Collectively we were all rather sad about it as we would have loved Scotland to get through as well but it was not to be. I would have been particularly happy if they had done so as my mother was a Scot.

Terry's tactical awareness on the day was second to none and the Dutch had no answer to the way England was playing. This was confirmed to me after the game by the great Sir Stanley Matthews, who came up looking for Terry in the VIP section. Stan was a guest of honour. He came up to me and said, 'Well done, Ted. Is Terry around?'

'Sorry, Stan, he's not around at the moment.'

'I have a car waiting to take me home so would you tell Terry that this was the finest England performance that I have ever seen and I would love to have played in it,' he said. It should be remembered that Stan was still playing football professionally at the age of fifty-one and was still coaching around the world into his late sixties. Not only was he a football legend but an absolute gentleman. He was never booked or sent off in his lifetime and for someone of his calibre to come up with that sort of remark was something special.

When I told Terry what he had said, I saw a bit of moisture in Terry's eyes and knew that meant something to him, coming from one of the all time greats.

While we were up in the VIP lounge after the game I was looking out for Frank de Boer to hand over his pennant but I couldn't see any sign of him. I asked Jordi Cruyff, another of their players, and he told me that Frank had already left so I held onto the pennant expecting him to catch up with me later. I never heard from him. Eventually I assumed that he didn't want a reminder of the Dutch defeat.

Some months later I received an invitation from the Chelsea Legends to go to a charity auction at Stamford Bridge. After my early years as a player with the Chelsea Metropolitan League, I had kept in touch with Ted Drake and Tom Smith, a close friend of his, who owned dogs with him and did a bit of scouting for Chelsea.

It was through them that I always got invited to the Chelsea Legends events. I even played for the Legends in a five-a-side tournament at Stamford Bridge when I was in my early fifties. So when I received a call asking me to support the charity, I thought of the pennant and decided that as Frank de Boer had expressed no further interest in it, I would donate it to the auction.

That event in 1997 was the first time I had an opportunity to have a good chat with John Terry, who was then a rising star at Chelsea. I was asked to explain the story behind the pennant and, when the bidding began, there was a lot of interest. The winning bid came from John Terry at £1000, which was quite a lot of money at the time. I admired him for digging deep into his pockets to support the charity and to this day wonder if he still has it. If Frank de Boer wants it, he'll have to get hold of John.

Our next game was against Spain but we didn't play at all well. The game was a bit of an anti-climax after the Dutch match. We only managed a 0–0 draw but we got through 4–2 on penalties through some great saves by David Seaman, so we were through to the semi-final.

It was against the old enemy, Germany. It was a terrific game with both teams performing well. Shearer scored in the first three minutes from a corner. Tony Adams had flicked it on with his head from the near post and Shearer came in and finished it. It was a great start but unfortunately Germany scored fifteen minutes later to equalise. Both sides had chances to win the game but in the last fifteen minutes we had two great chances to finish them off. Darren Anderton hit a post and then Gazza missed by literally an inch to get in on one of Alan Shearer's crosses and so it went to penalties.

The squad was totally confident that our five penalty-takers would all score and so they did. Perhaps we felt that David Seaman would save at least one of theirs. Unfortunately for us the Germans also scored all their five penalties as well so it came down to the sixth and final penalty. Paul Ince was down to take it but I think he had a calf strain and didn't want to so Gareth Southgate said he would have it. It turned out an easy save by the German keeper and so we lost out on a great chance of winning the European Cup, because I am confident we would have beaten the Czechs in the final, as Germany went on to do.

What has always haunted me is that I had already realised towards the end of the game that it was going into penalties and I thought we should take off Tony Adams, who had had injections before the game and in half time for an injured knee and was struggling. I thought we should have put on Nicky Barmby, who loved taking penalties, and I remain convinced that, if we had done that, he would have taken the sixth penalty and scored. I should have had the confidence to take Terry aside at that point to suggest it but I didn't. Who knows what the outcome would have been? But that's life and that's the game.

The atmosphere in the dressing room afterwards was understandably subdued as we were all disappointed with the outcome. It was also common knowledge that Terry's contract was coming to an end and that he had already told the FA that he would resign in the following January (1997) if they didn't extend his contract to take him through the World Cup qualifiers. Three members of the FA didn't want to extend his contract and Glenn Hoddle was being lined up to replace him.

Had we won the game against Germany and gone on to beat the Czechs in the final, public support for Terry would have pressurised the FA to renew his contract. As it was, we all knew that that would be our last game together as a team. Terry went around talking to each of the players and told them that they could go home that night if they wanted to.

Coming out of the stadium the roads were blocked with thousands of spectators and the police had a job to clear enough space for the coach to get through. The supporters were cheering us though so it seemed more like a victory parade than returning from a defeat and the crowds were still out to greet us as we drove through the security at Bisham Abbey. Many of the fans stayed outside overnight. The atmosphere must have influenced the players because, when we got back to Bisham, they all decided that they wanted to stay overnight and have a final get-together, so no one, staff or players, went home. We had a great evening reminiscing and reliving the game, enjoying the champagne that was set aside for a hoped-for victory.

In the morning everyone got their things together and players exchanged farewells. Alan Shearer gave me his shirt, which was signed by everyone, as did Jamie Redknapp. I still have the shirts in pride of place at home.

As I was loading the boot of my car, Steve McManaman, who later went on to play for Real Madrid, came over and gave me a big hug and said that it was the greatest England squad he had played in and that it was a pity that we couldn't have carried on under Terry as he was confident that we could have reached the finals of the World Cup. He asked me what I was going to do next and I explained that I still had a couple of months left on my contract with the FA, although Glenn Hoddle would be coming in with John Gorman. I told him I would wait to see what turned up.

'Promise me if you ever need anything at all just let me know,' he said.

I thought that was terrific and summed up the camaraderie that Terry had engendered among the entire squad. As it was, months later and after Steve had gone to Real Madrid, I needed a shirt for a charity do. I rang him up and asked if he could get me a shirt for the Heart Foundation. Within days I received a shirt by special delivery signed by all the Real Madrid team including Steve. It fetched over £2000 in the charity auction.

EASTWARD BOUND

I stayed at the FA for the last couple of months of 1996 to see out my contract but the atmosphere was not the same. Terry left straight after the tournament and Glenn Hoddle had taken his place. I knew that I would shortly be going and accepted that Glenn would bring in his own man.

I had stayed good friends with Peter Shreeves, who had earlier appointed me to Tottenham when I was at Gillingham, and I was pleased for him when he phoned me one night telling me that Glenn had asked him to join him at the FA. I assumed Peter would be offered my role and told him, 'It's a terrific job, Peter – the best job in the world.'

However a few weeks later Peter rang and asked me to meet him. He told me that Glenn had not mentioned anything more about the England job and instead had appointed John Gorman as his number two. Peter was clearly disappointed that he hadn't been offered a position and I don't know how the misunderstanding arose. Meanwhile, I effectively had no role as such and I knew they didn't really want me around.

But technically I had a few more weeks left at the FA. I was sent to look at potential players but I knew the crunch was coming as they were sending me to look at players that Terry and I would not normally have considered. Gorman asked me to go and see a boy playing for Queen's Park Rangers reserves to be considered for an under-21 England side. I thought Gorman was taking the piss as the boy was Scottish, so wouldn't play for England.

So I ignored that and booked myself in to Fulham to watch their game and discovered that Peter Taylor, who had been appointed by Glenn Hoddle as an under-21 coach, was also at the match. If the Queen's Park boy had been a serious prospect, Peter Taylor should have been sent to assess him, not me. When I got into the FA on the Monday morning, Gorman pulled me aside and said, 'Why didn't you go to see the boy at Queen's Park Rangers?'

'Because you're taking the piss and why didn't you send Peter Taylor who has just grassed on me?'

I never had too much respect for Peter Taylor after that. He's out in the Middle East now so our paths don't cross and in my opinion he never did too well with the clubs he managed in England. I would have had more respect for him if he had confronted me himself.

So I completed my contract with the FA and the staff were brilliant when I left. They put on a little reception for me, and Graham Kelly and David Davies both said they were sorry to see me go. 'I thought Glenn could have found you a job to do,' said Graham.

'That was never going to happen,' I said. I left on very good terms with them and remain friends with most of the staff. I still exchange Christmas cards with Michelle Farrar and Anne Romiley and am still on friendly terms with Glenn. He's a good coach and tactically aware. It's a pity that his time with England ended with controversy over negative publicity about his personal views.

After leaving England, Terry had taken over the Australian national team and he asked me if I wanted to go with him. I told him that I would see out my last weeks at the FA but I also told him that I had received a call from Andrew Croker, Ted Croker's son, who was working for the agency IMG. He asked if I wanted to take over as technical director at the Chinese national team. I had also already spoken to Tommy Lawrence at Strata because he was organising a tournament, the Dunhill Cup, in Malaysia, for the

▲ Me with Peter Barnes, Terry Venables, Dougie Livermore and Ray Clemence

▼ Walking onto the pitch at Wembley

▲ Me and Terry Venables at his club, Scribes

▼ With Terry and Jimmy Hill

With the Tottenham team, giving instructions to Pat Van Den Hauwe

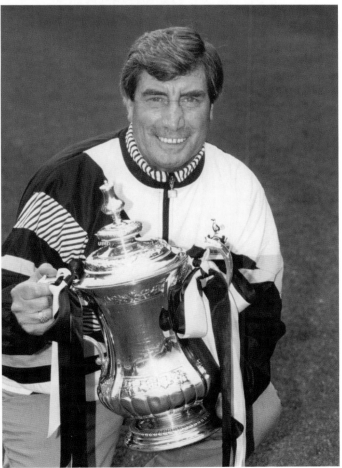

The FA Cup!

▲ Alan Shearer's signed shirt

▲ A signed Tottenham shirt, after winning the 1991 FA Cup against Nottingham Forest

▼ Me with Gazza, Dave Butler and Peter Beardsley

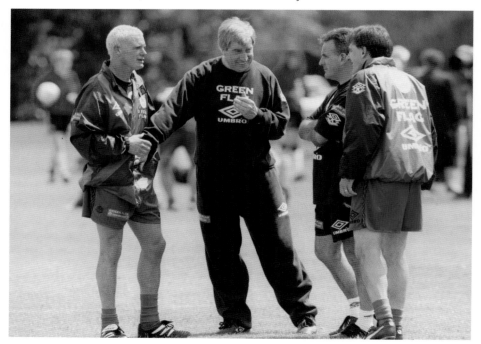

The 1994 England squad

The England squad at Euro '96

The World Cup Qualifiers in 1997

Invitations to Buckingham Palace and Downing Street

Tord Grip, Kenny Brown, David Beckham, Dave Sexton and me at Buckingham Palace

With coach Chie at the World Cup Asia Group, 1997

Millwall Legends

With Mark Robson, Gary Lineker and Gary Mabbutt at the Legends night in Tottenham

Chalfont St Peter FC

The Master of the Household

has received Her Majesty's command to invite

Mr. Ted Buxton

to a Reception to be given at Buckingham Palace by

The Queen

on Tuesday, 19th November, 2002 at 6.00 p.m.

to mark the 2002 World Cup

Dress: Lounge Suit

In Confirmation   Guests are asked to arrive between 5.30 and 5.50 p.m.

In recognition of the achievements of the England World Cup Squad 2002

The Prime Minister
and Mrs Blair

request the honour of the company of

Mr Ted Buxton

at a Reception at 10 Downing Street, Whitehall
Tuesday 8th October 2002, from 6.30 pm to 8.00 pm

An answer is requested to:
Laura Hester
Events & Visits Office
10 Downing Street
Whitehall, London SW1A 2AA
email: lhester@no10.x.gsi.gov.uk

This invitation is not transferable

With my sons and grandson, Jack

With my grand-daughters, Jade, Demi and Danielle

With my sons and grandsons, Joe and Jack

Chinese, prior to them going into the Asian Cup and the Oceanic qualifiers of the World Cup.

I told Terry I was interested in taking the China role because it would give me the chance to do something on my own. Terry was fully supportive and told me to go for it. He even said that it would be nice if both teams could get through the qualifiers as we might end up playing against each other. 'What a story that would be for the English press,' I said.

In September 1996 I accepted the Chinese job and in November flew via Zurich to Hong Kong, where I was to get a visa to travel into China. I arrived in Beijing at seven in the morning ready to watch my first game in Guangdong where China were to play Korea. They lost 3–2 to Korea. I then had to fly back to Hong Kong to get another visa, this time for Dubai, where they were to play Saudi Arabia in the next round of the Asian Cup.

I had a lot to sort out before I was to take over officially as technical director for the World Cup qualifiers. I had been introduced to the Chinese squad and coaches when they lost to Korea, as well as my interpreter, a small Chinese man of about forty. I think they called him Kim. Right from the start I was not too happy because I didn't think he could understand my cockney accent. I would be explaining to the players and the coaches the way I thought we should play after assessing the opposition, as well as writing on a flip chart and explaining different systems.

All the time the interpreter was shouting, 'Ha! Ha!' and saying something in Chinese as though he understood, but he didn't seem to be translating to the players and the coaches, who sat around looking bemused. Many of the Chinese lads understood what I was saying and two or three of them came to me afterwards and explained that the interpreter was getting it all wrong. I decided I needed a better interpreter. When I had a meeting with the officials they agreed and they had someone in mind, a young student studying English. He was a little chap, called Sammy, who spoke perfect English and stayed with me throughout my time in China. He used to run around with me on the pitch and, when I stopped the training to explain something to them, along with a few English swear words thrown in, Sammy would include the English swear words in his translation.

I soon discovered that a couple of the players could speak some English and one of them, a goalkeeper I only know as 'O', had picked up my rhyming slang. I found out when he came in with Jimmy Rimmer, who I had appointed as goalkeeping coach, after a hard training session and said, 'Ted, I'm fucking cream-crackered.'

The Chinese team got through to the quarter-finals of the Asian Cup but they failed to reach the semi-finals. As I didn't officially take charge until the Dunhill Cup and the World Cup qualifiers, I decided to get hold of a video tape of the Arsenal back five consisting of Seaman, Dixon, Adams, Bould and Winterburn, which under George Graham was one of the best defensive sides in the English League, to show the Chinese team how Arsenal were organised. They would move as a unit and played the manoeuvre to perfection. As it happened, the Arsenal side were also very mouthy towards the officials as soon as they spotted an opponent off side.

I showed the video to the Chinese team and they watched intently. I then put the team, together with the Chinese coaches, onto the training ground to try to get the team to perform as a unit, like Arsenal. After a few days working on it they started to get it but they were still keeping very quiet. So I told them to remember the video and how Bould and Adams, the central defenders at Arsenal, reacted. 'Tell them to get their fucking hands up and shout "off side" as soon as they succeed in manoeuvring the opponent into an off-side position,' I said to Sammy. Sammy gave them an excited explanation in Chinese with all of my swear words interspersed, along with a few extras of his own.

The players understood now and were playing exactly as I had instructed them. Unfortunately, from then on, whenever they spotted that an opponent was off side, they would shout out 'fucking' in English, followed by 'off side' in Chinese. It was hilarious but effective. I didn't worry too much, nor did the coaches, because no one else was likely to take offence as English was not widely spoken and they had now got the hang of the training system, which was what mattered. It didn't become an issue until many months later, after we had won the Dunhill Cup when I persuaded the Chinese FA that the team should come to England to play four friendlies. Knowing that swearing at the referees in England would not go down well, I had to take the team aside and impress on them that they had to limit their shouting to a simple 'off side', leaving out the colourful language.

My official role started with the Dunhill Cup, which was taking place in Kuala Lumpur in Malaysia. I was quite excited to be going back there as it was some forty-five years since I had spent my national service days fighting the Chinese insurgents in what was then Malaya. I had served with a regiment of the Gurkhas and now a group of serving Gurkha soldiers were appointed as our bodyguards. As soon as they saw that I had on my arm a tattoo from my service days depicting two crossed Gurkha kukris, the knives for which they are famous, they got quite excited and from then on treated me as one of them. We won the tournament unbeaten after trouncing Singapore 3–1, Finland 2–1, Malaysia 2–0 and then beating Bosnia 3–0 in the final. We also won the Fair Play Cup, which they award for the best-behaved team. I believe that was the first trophy they had won outside of China so it was a fantastic result.

Leaving the stadium for the hotel, I was sitting with Jimmy. Jim was a good lad and had been a very good keeper with Aston Villa and Arsenal. We got on well and I know the four Chinese goalkeepers all appreciated his work with them. We had a trophy each on our laps and I said, 'We'll have a bit of a celebration at the hotel with a few bottles of champagne.'

I told Sammy to let everyone know to be in the dining room at the hotel at the agreed time together with the officials from the Chinese FA and the coaches. We were not to be too late because Jimmy and I were due to fly back to England the following day to have a couple of weeks' break and the team was going back to Beijing.

Everything was arranged and Jimmy and I sat waiting for everyone to join us. About an hour after the designated time, no one had arrived. I got hold of one of the officials in his room and Sammy explained that they had all gone to bed because they had been instructed by the officials and their doctors that they should go straight to bed and, being disciplined, they had done just that. Sammy explained that they would look forward to seeing us back in China ready for the World Cup qualifiers.

Jimmy and I had a quiet night sharing a bottle of champagne on our own and went to bed as we had to be up at six o'clock the following morning to go to the airport. When we got out of the car at the airport, who should be there to greet us but the entire Chinese team with their staff and the officials standing as a guard of honour to see us off. As we walked through they were all clapping. It was an amazing experience and completed unexpected to have a send-off like that.

I am sure that it was the success of our Malaysian tournament that convinced the Chinese FA to agree to my suggestion that they should come to England to play a few friendlies and to gain experience against English clubs. I returned to the UK with Jimmy Rimmer with permission from the Chinese FA to arrange a series of friendly matches and to arrange a reasonable hotel close to the London venues. I got in touch with Keith Peacock, who was now back at his old club Charlton Athletic, and he put me in touch with a four-star hotel near Colchester, which was willing to accommodate the team at an acceptable rate. I had arranged to play Nottingham Forest, Charlton, Chelsea, Crystal Palace and Arsenal.

EASTWARD BOUND

A few days before the team was due to arrive I received a call from Sammy to say that the Chinese FA was not happy with the hotel arrangements because apparently the authorities considered it too luxurious and a distraction for the team. They could not be dissuaded so now I had to get hold of Keith again to try to make alternative arrangements, without which there would have been a real risk that the Chinese FA would pull out. Keith put us in touch with a local council that were able to put us up in a dormitory-style arrangement at a local school with catering facilities, even though the team brought their own chef with them. At least the location was convenient for training at Charlton's training ground.

The team flew over and Jimmy and I went to meet them at the airport. After they settled in at the dormitory, we had two days of training before we travelled to Nottingham Forest for our first game. Frank Clarke, the manager at Nottingham Forest, looked after us very well, although we beat them 4–1. I think he was quite impressed with the way we played. We went on to beat Charlton 2–0 and then thumped Chelsea 3–1. The most memorable games were the last two, because we decided to play the fringe players against Crystal Palace plus those who had returned from injury. Despite our previous good run we found ourselves 2–0 down at half time. The problem was that Ray Wilkins, who we all knew as Butch, a great player formerly with Chelsea, Manchester United and AC Milan, was now player-coach at Crystal Palace and he was absolutely on top of the game. Our young lads couldn't handle him.

After a long chat with the Chinese coaches I persuaded them to put all of their best players back on at half time because the Chinese would not have been happy to lose, even though this was only a friendly match. Pointing at Wilkins, I said to Sun Jihai, one of our midfield players, 'Sun, you have got to fucking stop him playing. Fucking rattle into him. Get tight to him and don't let him get his bloody head up to pass the ball.'

Sammy translated what I said into Chinese but, presumably as there were no equivalents in the language, he kept in the swear words. I couldn't help but smile to hear a torrent of Chinese interspersed with 'fucking' and 'bloody'.

We pushed further up the field to narrow the space in the middle of the park, which gave us more chance to get close to their midfield players. Sun certainly did his job because he was rattling into Wilkins and everybody else. We pulled back the two goals and went on to win 5–2.

When we went 3–2 ahead, Ray Wilkins decided to sub himself. He was probably annoyed with me because of my language on the touch line. As he walked off he came over to me and said, 'You're a fucking disgrace. That's the way you used to play. Are you planning to kick your way into the World Cup?'

'Fuck off, Ray. Behave yourself. I'll do what it takes to win,' I said.

Over the years since then Ray has of course moved on, done well on the management side at Chelsea and is a very good TV pundit. We get on well now and, when we are together, he often reminds people about that match and our altercation. I think he enjoys recounting the story.

The last game before returning to China for the World Cup qualifiers was against Arsenal. It got quite physical. Don Howe, my old colleague from the England squad, was in charge of the Arsenal team together with George Armstrong. Tackles were flying around and one of the Arsenal lads went over the top into a tackle on one of the Chinese lads, Li Tie, who was later to go to Everton.

All hell broke loose. Punches were thrown and all the players started to pile into each other. Don and George Armstrong and I waded in to the players to try to separate them. The referee, Ken Goldman (now Vice Chairman and Treasurer of the London Football Coaches Association), was a bit concerned and Don and

I decided that with only ten minutes left of the game we would leave it at that.

The referee was relieved when we said that, so we settled on a 0–0 draw, which satisfied the Chinese team and their officials because they ended the tour unbeaten. Arsenal gave us a nice reception after the game and it all ended well. So we successfully completed the Chinese team's first tour.

AN EASTERN EYE

The Chinese FA was very reluctant to let their players sign for English clubs because they were anxious that they should not be seen to fail. After the World Cup and after I had left China and joined Terry Venables at Crystal Palace, it took me some time to persuade the Chinese FA that their players should be allowed to join English clubs and that they would be successful. After a lot of negotiations, a fee for both players was agreed through Tommy Lawrence, the agent at Strata, for Sun Jihai from Dalian Wanda and Fan Zhiyi, the Chinese captain from Shanghai, to join Crystal Palace.

Sun Jihai turned out to be one of China's greatest players and went on to play for Manchester City and Sheffield United. He married his childhood sweetheart and settled in England where both of their daughters were born. We still keep in touch and he appreciates the opportunities he had. Fan Zhiyi did well too but eventually decided to return to Shanghai where he is now the manager coach at Shanghai East Asia.

After success in both Malaysia and England, our next task would be the World Cup qualifiers. The first game was in Turkmenistan. We set off from Beijing and were told that the flight would take four hours. And so, after four hours flying I assumed we had reached our destination only to be told by Sammy that we were in fact in Mongolia and had been diverted there because our visas had to be inspected.

I wasn't too happy, especially as first-class travel on the Chinese airline at that time was hardly what we would consider first class. I was even less happy when the Mongolian guards came on the plane and we were shuffled off into the shed that they called their terminal where our passports and visas were examined. We were then escorted straight back to our plane where the guards suddenly presented the team with footballs and pennants to sign. I suspected that this was the only reason for our diversion so I told Sammy to tell the team to sign and get it done with so that we could be on our way. We then had a further four hours to get to Turkmenistan.

Turkmenistan is on the border with Afghanistan, which was already in turmoil. The Russians strictly patrolled the border with Afghanistan to stop drugs entering the Russian market. We discovered this after we had arrived late that night at the hotel and all the players and Jimmy Rimmer, the officials and I had finally sat down to have something to eat and to relax after the journey.

It was about midnight when, as we were sitting on the balcony where the officials were smoking their cigarettes, the still of the night was broken by the sound of gunfire. One of our Russian security guards ordered us to get back inside and explained that they were firing on drug smugglers coming over the border. I turned to the Chinese officials and Jimmy and said, 'What a way to start the World Cup. It's like being in a bloody war zone.'

The facilities at the training ground were pretty basic and the pitches were very poor but nonetheless the Chinese team adapted quickly to the conditions and we won the game 4–1. To be fair, the Turkmenistan officials treated us quite well at the reception afterwards.

We flew straight from there to Uzbekistan. The Russian police were looking after the team and a Russian was allocated to look after Jimmy and me. He was short for a Russian and reminded me of Charles Aznavour, the famous French singer, so I called him Charlie. I left the hotel alone to stretch my legs shortly after the flight and walked towards a park, just across the road from the hotel. As I got to the park, Charlie came out from the hotel shouting at me, 'Coach! Coach!' in his broken English.

He said that I should never go anywhere alone in this place and at that point a dark limousine with blacked-out windows drew up a short distance away and two big heavies got out. They stood there staring at me. I was sure that Charlie had a gun under his coat. He said something to them in Russian and they got back in the car and drove off. He pointed to my rings and the gold chain round my neck and waved his finger in front of my face, saying, 'No. No more.'

We went back to the hotel. Jimmy was still sitting with the officials having cigarettes so I told Sammy what had happened and he relayed it to the Chinese. They said I should have been told before we came about how dangerous some of these places were but it's only when you experience these situations in person that you appreciate the risks.

On the day of the game it was my sixty-third birthday, 11 May 1997. The Chinese officials gave me what they described as a bottle of champagne to celebrate but, far from a champagne of the best vintage, it turned out to be a bottle of fizzy blackcurrant. We didn't play particularly well but we managed to win the game 1–0, which kept up the momentum.

The next game was two weeks later in Vietnam so we had a couple of friendlies against local sides in Ho Chi Minh City. We had a terrific welcome there and the hotel was superb. The catering manageress, a Vietnamese girl who spoke perfect English, told me that she had two sons but had lost her husband in the Vietnam war. She kept hinting about going to America to see her mother and asked me to send her a picture of my house in England once I had returned home.

I forgot all about it until about a month later when I was back in England for a break. I was with Eric Hall, the agent, who had asked me to go with him to negotiate a deal for a player to go to Wimbledon. We drove past Buckingham Palace. In those days you could drive directly in front of the gates and the police on duty were not too troubled when I got Eric to stop and take a photograph of me leaning against the gate at Buckingham Palace. I sent the photo to the girl in Vietnam. When I returned again to England after the end of the World Cup qualifiers, I received a letter from her saying how much she liked my house and asking for money for her to go to America.

During the qualifiers, the team played well and we won the game in Vietnam 3–1. The weather was beautiful and we had a few days' break in Ho Chi Minh City before flying back to Beijing. The officials and the coaches insisted that during that break they wanted the players to train. I wanted them to rest for three days. After quite a lot of arguments with the officials, I arranged for the management to let us have the swimming pool to ourselves and to put two water polo goals in the pool and convinced the coaches and officials that this was a good compromise to give them exercise and relaxation. I joined in the fun and invited Jimmy to join us but he made his excuses and said that he wanted to go to the silk market to buy a gift for his wife. He was planning to go with Sammy so I told them to be careful because Jimmy carried his money round his waist in a money belt.

A few hours later as I was relaxing with a bottle of wine, Jimmy returned looking decidedly dishevelled and distressed. He had been deliberately knocked down by a woman and a man on a motorcycle and as he lay on the ground she had leapt down and cut off his money belt with a knife. Sammy had apparently been distracted and separated from Jimmy. Jim lost about $1000 in various currencies so the mugger got off with a good haul and there was no present for his wife. I persuaded the officials to give him a loan of $500 to get him by but it put a dampener on our visit to Vietnam. Apart from that it had been a fascinating country where we met many interesting people and one I would have liked to have revisited.

In China we played the return game against Turkmenistan, which we won 1–0, and then had a disappointing game against Tajikistan, drawing 0–0. But then we beat Vietnam 4–0 in our last game before the next group stage.

I spent a few weeks back home in England and missed a few friendly games that China played in my absence. The coaches had assured me that I didn't need to be there and they got through the friendlies without too much trouble but afterwards I regretted that I hadn't spent the time with them because, in my absence, they had brought some young lads into the squad without my involvement.

When I got back for the first big home game against Iran, they had already decided to play a few of these lads in the match. With hindsight, that was a mistake as we went one up but then a few errors were made by the less experienced players and it was not until we were 3–1 down that I persuaded the coaches to change the line-up and bring on three experienced players who they had left out. We got back into the game and at 3–2 I thought we might make a comeback but a mistake by the keeper left us at 4–2.

I didn't endear myself to the coaches when I mentioned in the press conference after the game that they had been over-confident in putting on the young players against an experienced side like Iran. It has always been my policy to put on your best players if they are fit and I felt the coaches had been overly influenced by the performance of the young players in the friendly games, ignoring the fact that they were then up against lesser opponents. My comments were picked up by the Chinese press which then criticised me for missing the friendlies.

We then flew to Qatar, which at the time was a horrendous place, to play the next round. It was stiflingly hot and I had trouble even getting my breath, but despite the conditions, we achieved a 1–1 draw after the coaches took my advice and played their best team.

We won the next two games, 1–0 against Saudi Arabia in China and then back to Kuwait where we won 2–1. We were now well on our way to qualifying for the next round. I had stayed in touch with Terry and we speculated that both China and Australia were due to play Iran and, if both got through, Terry and I would have been on opposing sides, which would have made a great story and a memorable occasion for both of us and the British press.

Unfortunately, we flew into Iran for the return match with injuries and suspensions, so we had a few key players missing, including Fan Zhiyi, Hao Haidong, our leading goal scorer, and Xu Hung, who was one of the top defenders. We put in the young players again, such as Ling Min and Li Tie, who was only about sixteen and hadn't played an international game before.

We didn't get off to a good start in Iran. We came out to train on the first morning wearing our usual shorts and tracksuit tops, but were told in no uncertain terms that we were not allowed to show our legs. After a few heated words with the Iranian security, we had to go back and change into tracksuit bottoms, despite the heat.

Before the game, I was asked if I would like to go to see the palace of the Shah of Persia, who had been overthrown in the Islamic Revolution in 1979 and replaced by the Ayatollah Khomeini. It was an amazing place and they showed me the glass hallways where the Shah would go to visit his wife. Although the new republic despised the wealth of the previous regime, in one corner of the palace they were selling to visitors jewellery which they claimed to have confiscated from palace staff.

I picked up a gold ring that just fitted my little finger. The seller claimed that it had once belonged to the lady-in-waiting to Empress Farah and asked me, in reasonable English, for $400. Sammy was with me and he had been briefed to say when asked that I only had $100 on me. So when I said, 'Sammy, how much money do I have?' he immediately responded with '100 dollar' in an overly accented English.

I shrugged to the seller and said, '$100, that's it.' As we walked away, he shouted, ' OK, Coach, $100,' so I got the bargain and still wear the ring today.

It's a pity we didn't get such a good deal out of the game. There was a lot going against us. We had to contend with injuries and the young players playing their first games in front of more than 100 000 people in the searing heat. All round the stadium the Iranians had suspended massive posters showing portraits of the mullahs, which the players found very intimidating. At half time when we were already 2–0 down, all the spectators suddenly started praying as it was their prayer time. They were still deep in salah, as it is called, when we walked back onto the pitch. We had made a few tactical changes at half time, hoping to improve, but we eventually lost 4–1. Obviously the prayers had worked for them.

The next game was against Qatar in the Workers' Stadium in Beijing. We needed to win and were expected to win but unfortunately I had to fly back to England to have an operation to remove a cyst. It was in a delicate place and I didn't want to run the risk of being gelded in China through a mistranslation.

While I was recovering at home before the game, I got a call from Jimmy Rimmer and Sammy in which they told me that the Chinese were going to make wholesale changes in the line-up for the game against Qatar. Jimmy told me they thought it was time to put the young players back in and they were even planning to play the second-string goalkeeper.

I went ballistic and told them this would be suicide as we had to win this game and needed our best side to stay in contention. I stressed to Jimmy that he had to stand up for what we believed would be the strongest side. But it was to no avail. They went ahead despite my protestations and they lost 3–2, much to the disappointment of the Chinese nation. It now looked doubtful that we would be able to qualify.

To stay in the tournament, we needed to win the next game, which was against Saudi Arabia in their home country. I flew straight out from Heathrow and was picked up by the kitman and my interpreter. The Saudis were very well organised and the training facilities were brilliant. The Chinese lads and the officials had a chef cooking all their own Chinese food. Jimmy and I had another chef cooking steaks for us.

The following day after training, the head of the Chinese contingent, who was also a former national coach and spoke excellent English, confirmed that I had to attend the press conference that evening. I protested that the coach should go but he insisted that I should go and that I should wear a jacket, not my usual training gear. I only had my England blazer with me with the three English lions on it but he insisted that this would be fine. At the scheduled time I walked into the conference room of the stadium. It was very luxurious by our standards with plush armchair-style seating and fruit and refreshments laid out, although no alcohol of course.

The Arabs, dressed in their robes, were very polite and greeted me with a bow and handshake. I felt as if I had stepped onto the set of the *Arabian Nights*. They had previously told me that we had an English referee coming and I hadn't thought too much about it when the doors opened and in came David Elleray, one of the top referees in England, along with his linesmen. As soon as he walked in he saw me, came straight over to me and greeted me like an old friend as he had refereed a number of our games at Tottenham and England. I noticed then that the Arabs seemed to become a little more aloof.

It transpired that David Elleray was the first Englishman to referee a game between Saudi Arabia and China and so, after the meeting, David came over and asked me if there was any chance that I could get four shirts as a memento of the occasion for him and his assistants. I told him that this might be awkward but I would do what I could. I got hold of the Chinese kitman and relayed the request to him through Sammy. I could tell by Sammy's tone that he was impressing on the kitman that it was important.

At the start of the game the next day, the groundsman and Sammy came to me with four shirts stuffed into a paper bag. As we had to give the team sheets to the referee an hour before the game, I told Sammy to come with me and bring the bag. When we got there, we found two Arabs standing each side of the referee's door. I suspect that they had been put there because the Arabs suspected something underhand was going on but I couldn't explain to them that swapping a few shirts as a memento was not going to influence the referee.

They let me though with the team sheet accompanied by one of the Chinese coaches. Sammy started to follow me in but was blocked by the two guards, who were obviously aware of what was going on. I got a bit annoyed at the guards and pointed to the bag, gesticulating that it belonged to the referee. Sammy was saying much the same but the guards would not let him through so I took the bag from Sammy and went into the referee's room. The guards didn't try to stop me.

David was delighted with their mementos. We had a short chat about the 1994–96 European Championship and I wished him well for the game and said we would meet up later whatever the outcome.

The game was quite physical with a hot tempo both on and off the field. We went in front 1–0 until he awarded the Saudis a penalty, which I considered to be a soft penalty as I don't think our lad had made contact with the Saudi player. They scored from the penalty and the game finished 1–1, which was no good for either team because we both needed a win to have any hope of progressing. At the reception afterwards, I went over to David and his entourage, put on a mock disgruntled expression and said, 'That

was a diabolical penalty you gave them – I want those shirts back.'
He must have found the incident amusing because he mentioned
it when he wrote a book some years later.

It was particularly disappointing for me because I had hoped
that if we got through we would have had the chance to play against
Australia. As it turned out things didn't go Terry's way either.

The Australians needed to win the game against Iran in
Melbourne. They were already 2–0 up and looked like winning the
game with twenty minutes to go when fans ran onto the pitch. They
pulled the nets down from the goal at one end and consequently
the game had to be delayed for about half an hour while the goal
was repaired and the crowd returned to their seats.

At that point, the Aussies looked to be well on top with the
prospect of going into the World Cup qualifiers but after the
interruption they seemed to lose their momentum. The Iranians
scored two goals, in the last twenty minutes to equalise and then
went through on away goals so Australia, like China, was out of
the World Cup and Terry and I never again got the chance of
our teams playing against each other. That would have been some
match but it was not to be.

After the Saudi game, we returned to Beijing where the squad
got together at a hotel with the representatives from the Chinese
Football Association where we had a debriefing and talked about
developing the future for the team. They were clearly disappointed
about how the game had gone but the Chinese Football Association
had taken on board my previous advice about building the team
and coping with disappointment, so there were no recriminations
and they were looking to the future.

The Chinese press were much more critical and there was a lot
in the media about the quality of the coaches and the ages of the
players, but when I talked to them I pointed out that we had been
hampered by injuries and the fact that some of our best players were
suspended and that we had a lot of good young players coming

through so the prospects for the future were very encouraging. According to Sammy, who read the papers the next day, the press seemed to have been very responsive to what I had said.

My contract with China was due to end with the World Cup so it was mutually agreed that I would return home later that week. Jimmy Rimmer had been offered a job as goalkeeping coach at Dalian Shide in Guangzhou so he was staying on in China.

A few months later when I was back in England I was surprised to receive a call from Jimmy's wife telling me that Jimmy had met a Canadian girl who was teaching English in China and that he had left his wife and family to stay out there. It was the first I had heard of it and took me quite by surprise because Jimmy had always seemed such a family man. I think his wife blamed me to some extent for having taken him to China but at the time they had both been pleased that I had got him the job. No one was to know how events would turn out. I understand that he is now coaching in Canada but I haven't been in touch with him since I left him in China.

BACK TO BLIGHTY – PART TWO

Once I got back to the UK in 1998, I joined Bobby Robson and Charlie Woods, his number two, at Newcastle on a part-time basis to do assessments and team reports. Bobby was an extraordinary man and one of the nicest people I have ever met. I had known him over the years through coaching courses and we had often spoken about certain players. When I was with Tottenham and out in Portugal assessing Portuguese players, Bobby was with Sporting Clube de Portugal and then Porto. When he was with Porto he had introduced me to his young interpreter, Jose Mourinho, who has of course gone on to become one of the world's best coaches. I can understand how he achieved that, having gained so much experience working with Bobby in Portugal and then in Barcelona. When I received the call from Charlie Woods, I jumped at the chance to work with Bobby.

One of my first assignments was to go and do a team report on Middlesbrough, one of their north-east rivals. I wrote the report as normal, gave it to Bobby and thought no more of it. I had put down a few aspects that I considered to be Middlesbrough's weaknesses and suggested what system I thought should be played against them. Newcastle subsequently beat Middlesbrough at Middlesbrough. I then got a call from Charlie to say that Bobby wanted me to spend a weekend with them in Newcastle where they were to play a game against Everton at St James's Park.

Paul Gascoigne was now playing for Everton so I got the strong impression that Bobby realised it would be nice for me to meet up again with Paul and his family from Gateshead in the players' lounge after the Everton game. It was probably the first time we had had any time together since the end of the 1994–96 European Cup. Gazza looked well and was playing well despite having suffered a number of injuries over the years and so we had a nice hour catching up on old times. I always got on well with his dad, John, who was very close to Gazza.

Bobby and his staff then gathered in a conference room in the ground for a specially arranged session with a number of Newcastle supporters who had won a competition to participate in a question and answer session. One of the first comments from one of the supporters was to congratulate Bobby on the way the team had beaten Middlesbrough the week before.

Before he could go any further Bobby cut in and said, 'Let me stop you there because the credit is not all down to me. A large part of the credit belongs to that man sitting there.' He pointed to me. He introduced me to them as having worked with Terry Venables and then continued, 'He wrote the report on Middlesbrough and suggested a few ways we should play against them. I followed some of his suggestions and you all know how it worked out.' That was typical of the man's strong management skills. I felt a bit embarrassed when they all stood up and clapped but it was an emotional moment.

That evening we went to one of the restaurants in Newcastle's ground. There were Newcastle supporters there and other diners in the level above us; we were on the ground floor where the piano player was playing at a grand piano. After the meal we were finishing off with after-dinner drinks. The waiter had just delivered my port when Bobby said, 'I think we should hear Ted sing now.' He had heard me singing at Scribes.

I protested that we didn't have a mike or any props and I hadn't had a chance to warm up or prepare, but Bobby was insistent. Despite my protests, he kept trying to persuade me, saying, 'Come on, you can do it.' He egged on the audience saying, 'We all want to hear him, don't we?'

The piano player said he would tinkle around with a few tunes to get me started so I found myself caught up with the moment and I didn't want to refuse Bobby after the compliments he had paid me earlier in the afternoon. At one point I said jokingly to the audience, 'Sinatra never had this pressure.'

'Let's hear you,' called Charlie Woods.

I looked around and Bobby's P.A., Judith, gave me a smile so I looked at the piano player and asked, 'Can you play, *All The Way?*' It was from the film *The Joker Is Wild*, the biography of Joe E. Lewis. In the film Frank Sinatra sings the song to Jeannie Crain so I sang the song to Judith.

It well down well with my audience and everyone clapped but Charlie brought me back down to earth with his shout of, 'I think you're better doing team reports so don't give up your day job.' This got an even bigger round of applause.

I was still working for Bobby when I went to Wembley in October 2002 to watch some of the individual players for both sides in the England match against Germany in the last game to be played in the old Wembley stadium before it was to be demolished and rebuilt. England lost the game 1–0. Afterwards I was in the VIP lounge when Kevin Keegan, the England manager, came in after taking a press conference.

Prior to the game he had already had a lot of flak from the media and certainly had been given a tough time at the press conference. There had been some speculation in the papers that the FA might bring Terry Venables back as England manager. When Kevin walked in from the press conference, looking very agitated, he spotted me and came over and pulled me aside. 'If Terry wants this fucking job, he's welcome to it,' he snapped. 'I don't need all this stick.'

I felt for him because so many England managers have been through the same scenario, so I told him to go home and take Jean, his wife, out for a meal and then think things over quietly.

Shortly afterwards, Kevin resigned from the England job. The speculation in the press then intensified and I did wonder if Terry would be offered the job because he still had a lot of supporters. I would have been pleased if that had happened as I would have hoped that I would be able to rejoin him there.

However, on my next visit to Newcastle, Bobby took me aside and told me that he had been offered the England job following Kevin's resignation. I was equally pleased that it had been offered to Bobby as either he or Terry would have been a great choice. Both were popular with the fans and players alike. Bobby told me that he would like to take the job but he didn't think Newcastle would allow him to do so, even on a part-time basis. That turned out to be the case, so neither Terry nor Bobby got it and Peter Taylor was put in charge until Sven-Göran Eriksson was appointed, which came as something of a surprise to most people.

Meanwhile I got a call from Sam Hammam, the chairman of Wimbledon, asking me to join the club. 'Have you spoken to [Wimbledon manager] Joe Kinnear about me?' I asked.

He said of course he had and that Joe would phone me. Joe didn't call so a week later Sam rang again and asked if Joe had been in touch. When I said that he hadn't, Sam said that he would be the next day. Joe did eventually call me and arranged to meet me at the Wimbledon training ground off the A3 in Surrey. We went across to a pub and agreed terms and went back and signed a contract for one year. I had the distinct feeling that I was the chairman's appointment and not Joe's so it didn't feel entirely right to me and I was not overly enthusiastic but it was the only full-time offer on the table at the time, because my role at Newcastle with Bobby was only part-time.

Besides which, it was the old crazy gang at Wimbledon – Vinny Jones, Dennis Wise, Ben Thatcher, Lawrie Sanchez, and Mick Harford. When I drove into the training ground on my first day I got hold of Lawrie and David Kemp, who was Joe's number two, knowing that any new players or staff who joined Wimbledon could expect an initiation ritual, at which they either punctured the tyres on your car, cut your clothes up or played some similar trick.

So I told them, 'If I have any problems, you'll have more trouble than you can handle from me.'

I think the word was put out because I never had any problems with them. In fact, when I sat down with the team one day after training, a few of the lads were looking at the *Racing Post* when I picked up the paper and casually mentioned a horse and said, 'This is a good each way bet.'

I thought no more about it until I got a phone call that night from Neal Ardley, one of the players: 'That was a good shout, Ted, It came in at 25 to 1.'

I was amazed as it was just a quick glance at the paper but it had obviously been noted and had gone down well. After that, the players constantly asked me for tips but I would tell them it was a one-off. At least I had their attention and never had any problems. Mick Harford and David Kemp were great with me on the training field but I did notice that whenever I was out with the players, Joe never came out.

Crystal Palace and Wimbledon were sharing the grounds at Selhurst Park. It was a few months later that Terry took over at Crystal Palace. I had been on a few trips to Norway with Sam Hammam, one in which we had taken a private helicopter to attend a meeting with some Norwegian businessmen. I suspected that Sam was either trying to sell the club or to get investors to buy into it. I had the distinct feeling that if they did take over they would bring in their own coaches. I told Joe Kinnear when I got back what had happened and he didn't seem too concerned and said he could handle it. So I left it with him.

By now I was starting to feel that my initial concerns about joining Wimbledon were justified and that Joe really didn't want me there. When I had agreed terms with Sam, he had asked me, 'If Terry gets another job, would you go with him?'

'No, if I am satisfied with where I am, I would stay,' I said.

Consequently, when I received a call from Terry asking me to join him at Crystal Palace in March 1998, I told Terry what I had agreed with Sam and that he would thus have to ring Sam and talk to him directly. I then got a call at home that night from Sam and he said, 'I've spoken to Terry and told him that I don't want you to go.'

'I know I promised you, Sam, but just let me talk to Terry first,' I said.

'You tell me now,' he said. 'Stay or go but you've got to tell me now.'

I started to feel a bit angry and felt that he was putting a gun to my head. So I told him, 'Now you put it like that, I'll go.' So I agreed to join Terry at Crystal Palace, which had recently been taken over by Mark Goldberg.

About a week later I got a nice letter from Sam Hammam, which I still have, saying that he was sorry about how we had ended and that he understood the good relationship I had with Terry. He also understood my decision to leave Wimbledon to go with him. Over the years since, we have occasionally met to have a drink together, mainly at the Landmark London Hotel in Marylebone, and we have always stayed on good terms.

I met with Terry and Mark Goldberg to agree everything with them about my appointment as assistant to Terry and chief scout. Terry Fenwick and Dave Butler, who had been with us in Tottenham, were also taken on; Terry as coach and Dave as physio. It looked a great set-up at the time and Mark had major ambitions for the club. He first arranged a meeting with all the players and it was very professionally organised. He also arranged an open day at the ground for the fans to come in and meet everyone and ask questions. When Mark called me and Terry into his office after these sessions, he looked at us and said, 'I'm going to give you £15 million to spend on players. Do you think you can get us promotion?'

To which I said with all the confidence in the world, 'Well, if we don't, you'll have to sack us.'

One of my first signings for Crystal Palace came after Tommy Lawrence had recommended to Terry a midfield player with Elfsborg in Sweden. Terry decided that I should fly to Sweden to have a look. I was met at the airport by the Swedish agent and taken to the game but, having watched the player, I realised early on he was no better than others we already had at Crystal Palace. However, the one who impressed me was another player, Mathias Svensson, a blond striker over six foot tall with good technical ability and a sweet left foot.

I thought his physical presence would be suited to the English league so I phoned Tommy Lawrence and told him that I thought the centre forward would be good enough for Crystal Palace.

Tommy negotiated with Terry to get the boy over and started negotiations directly with the player as he had not signed with an agent. Matt Svensson turned out to be a good signing for the club. He was very popular with the Crystal Palace crowd, scoring vital goals and went on to be player of the year. Later he went on to win three international caps for Sweden before retiring with a knee injury. We still keep in touch.

Unfortunately, Mark Goldberg's ideas were over ambitious and he was also spending extravagantly on extras like computer experts and technology, as well as overpaying some of the players against Terry's advice. Terry raised concerns about the level of expenditure within the first year and mentioned to me that it would have to be brought under control or the club would be in difficulties.

Some weeks later, Terry phoned me, Terry Fenwick and Dave Butler in the morning before we were due to go to a training session and asked us to meet him in London. I knew as soon as I took the call that something was up because Terry would not normally ask us to miss a training session and I was therefore apprehensive that this would be bad news. As soon as we got together, my fears were confirmed when Terry told us that he was finished with the club, as we all were. It was all ending and the club would be going into administration.

Terry was clearly troubled and probably more upset because he felt responsible for having brought us all in. Terry and Dave had also given up full-time positions to join Crystal Palace. None of us blamed Terry because it was a choice made of our own free will to join him and Terry had done his best to make it a success. Football is a game of incredible highs and crashing lows so you have to learn to roll with the punches.

So our relationship with the club finished abruptly with Terry leaving in January 1999 and my leaving at the end of the season. It was still operating under Attilio Lombardo, who had been put in temporary charge with John Cartwright, the youth team manager, as the first team coach. All the senior staff had gone and the club was just playing out the season with the administrators handling its affairs. It was a desolate atmosphere in comparison to the high hopes we had had at the beginning.

Steve Coppell, who was a director of the club, was interviewed on BBC radio about the club going into administration and he said that the one he felt most sorry for was Ted Buxton, which I understood was because I had been so totally committed to Crystal Palace.

Terry had assured us that we would be paid up to the end of the month but this still left a question mark over the amount due under our contracts. Terry Fenwick and Terry Venables reached a settlement but Dave Butler and I were left attending frequent creditors' meetings when the administrators presented their figures on the club's assets and liabilities and what payments would be made and what would be prioritised.

Dave and I were clearly not at the top of the list and it took nine more years before we finally received a payment that was eventually less than half of what was owed. After that length of time and having been told by the administrators that we had little hope of receiving anything, we had virtually given up all hope of getting our money so it came as quite a pleasant surprise when one of the administrators with whom I had regular contact called to tell me that I would finally be receiving a part-payment. To be fair to Mark Goldberg, he had worked hard to find the money and I believe this payment only came about because he had put extra money into the administration.

Now of course the club is back on its feet and doing well and Mark is managing Bromley Football Club and enjoying himself there. One of my grandsons, Joe, is a supporter of Millwall and of Bromley and gives me regular updates on Bromley's performance. Joe and his brother, Jack, are my son Vince's boys. Jack was a promising young player for Millwall and did some training at Bromley until he suffered a bad leg injury that prevented him pursuing a footballing career.

HE'S ONLY BEING MODEST

Soon after I left Crystal Palace I received a call from a publisher saying that they thought I should write a book on soccer training and asking if I would be interested. Keen as I was, I didn't know anything about putting a book together but they provided two expert helpers and we spent many summer days in Hyde Park working on the text and illustrations.

The book was published in 2000 and I was surprised to see recently that copies are still being sold and resold around the world and it has been translated into numerous other languages. I didn't get paid much for doing it but I got a kick out of seeing it in print, especially when people like Lawrie McMenemy and David Pleat mentioned that they had seen it on sale as far afield as the US and Canada.

During the following months I was busy doing scouting and assessment jobs for various clubs. In the course of one of those games I sat with Dave Sexton, who was then on the coaching staff with Sven-Göran Eriksson and was monitoring players for the England squad. He asked me what I was doing and I mentioned that, although I was busy with different clubs, I wanted to find a more regular role. He said he was sure that something would turn up and I thought nothing more of it.

A few weeks later I received a call from Dave out of the blue asking if I fancied going back to the FA to work on scouting and assessment for England prior to the 2002 World Cup. They would also be monitoring the teams in the Confederation Cup because they would be expecting to face Korea, Japan, and Australia and some of the other Asian sides during the World Cup.

After Dave's call, Michelle Farrar, the then international secretary at the FA who subsequently completed thirty-one years with the FA, followed up to arrange a meeting with Sven, Tord Grip, his number two and Michelle herself. It was the first time I had met Sven and Tord Grip and they asked me a lot of questions about certain players and how much I knew about the Far East.

They enquired as to whether I would be prepared to go to Korea and Japan to assess the facilities and liaise with the Australian national team in preparation for the England national team to go out there for the World Cup. The Australian national team were competing in the Confederation Cup. I jumped at the chance to get back to work with England and with the new team coming in, which had a lot of potential. I was particularly looking forward to working with the new management team and with Sven, who had a completely different style of coaching from Terry. I was quite excited at the prospect of working in Asia and meeting up with the Socceroos.

Arrangements were made for me to fly out to Korea with the Swedish doctor who Sven had taken on board. We flew to Inchon via Amsterdam to meet up with the Aussies at their hotel. It was great to meet them again as I already knew a lot of the Australian players who had joined us at Crystal Palace and Portsmouth and had since returned to play with their national team. It was the first time that I had met the Australian coach Frank Farina and his assistant Dave Phillips, who were both very welcoming and made me feel as if I were part of their squad.

The Australian lads seemed very relaxed but they worked hard and played hard. Back in the hotel there was a lot of banter and reminiscences about our exploits in the previous World Cup when the Australian and Chinese teams had both been beaten by Iran. One morning, during a break while the players were getting some fluids down them, I was out on the training field talking to Frank Farina about tactics of play. I heard a familiar French accent behind me. 'Mr Buxton, could I have a word?'

I recognised the distinctive voice from TV interviews and turned round, but it was the first time I had met Arsène Wenger, who had recently been appointed as Arsenal manager. He was obviously in Korea to monitor the players, which is very much in keeping with his hands-on style of management, making sure he thoroughly understood the background of his players.

After I had introduced him to Frank Farina and the Swedish doctor, Arsène Wenger pulled me aside and asked if I could tell him about Sol Campbell, who we had signed as a schoolboy and who went on to play for England. I asked him what he wanted to know as he already knew what Sol could do as a player.

He replied, 'I know what he can do as a player, I want to know about him as a man.'

I told him that we had signed him to Tottenham as a fourteen-year-old schoolboy. He was from a large Jamaican family and as a youngster Sol's timekeeping had been poor when he came into training. John Moncur, our youth development officer at Tottenham, knew what potential Sol had and had taught him to be more disciplined. As he developed, he worked hard at his game but for such a big man he was very quiet. He hardly ever spoke and tended to withdraw into himself. In his early days I also felt that he had been reluctant to play if he wasn't 100 per cent fit, but that he had overcome that and gained in confidence as the years went on. 'You know he is a great player, he's a solid man to have in the team,' I said.

Arsène was very grateful for the information. Soon afterwards he brought Sol from Tottenham and because of the rivalry between the two clubs, I thought it was a brave decision by Wenger because he had to be sure that Sol had the inner strength to cope with criticism from the Tottenham fans. I only occasionally meet

Arsène Wenger, either at the Emirates Stadium or at away games but, if he sees me, he always makes a point of coming for a chat and to shake hands, even if only briefly. I feel he appreciated that exchange we had in Korea and I understand why he'll always be a legend at Arsenal.

I was travelling to one game after another and it was exhausting to get from one city to the next, checking into different hotels and journeying mostly on the excellent Korean trains. I would be up all night after each game writing reports and faxing them to the England headquarters and then catching the train to the next match the following day.

The US–Mexico game in Jeonju was a funny one. I was in a train carriage with a group of Mexicans sitting by the window enjoying watching the countryside and the workers in the paddy fields handling their cattle. It reminded me of my time in Malaya except that I was now in a designated air-conditioned seat and no one was lying in wait to fire at me.

It had been a quiet and pleasant journey until we pulled into the station that was right beside the stadium. As the train stopped, a big American with the stars and stripes flag draped around his shoulders ran down from another carriage. As he got to the electric doors that opened up he jumped around to face all the Mexicans and bellowed, 'Remember the Alamo!'

There was a deathly silence and I thought that this was going to get nasty. Then a Mexican stood up from his seat further along the carriage and said in perfect English, 'Yes pal, we fucked you there as well.' The American didn't know what to say so, as the carriage doors opened again, he jumped off. All the Mexicans started clapping, and I joined in because I thought it was brilliant. As it was, the US won the game 2–0 so I suppose the American got the last laugh.

One of the most memorable games in the knock-out stage was South Korea beating Italy 2–1 in Daejeon. The refereeing was very controversial with questionable decisions by the Ecuadorian referee against the Italians, a scandal that had been a factor in a number of games that resulted in teams that were predicted to do well being eliminated

The Koreans hadn't expected to win so they went crazy with excitement, resulting in chaos in the stadium and the surrounding streets. It took me hours to get out to meet the taxi driver who had taken me there and had arranged to wait for me after the game. I had to fight my way through the crowds of Koreans going mad and arrived at the spot where the he was due to meet me. I never thought he would be there but found that he had locked himself in his cab because people were trying to get inside in the excitement.

He saw me and his face lit up. He opened the door, shoved me in saying something excitedly in Korean and drove me back to the hotel through all the crowds thronging the streets all the way back through the city. I really appreciated that he had waited so long for me but I was presumably paying him a lot more than his normal fares. I got back to the hotel, completely exhausted, had a glass of wine and wrote my report on the South Korean team and faxed it to the England management team who were then based in their hotel in Japan.

England beat Denmark and were through to the quarter-finals, in which we would play Brazil. In the meantime, I went to Gwangju to watch South Korea play against Spain. That was another long day but by the time the game took place, England had already been eliminated the night before by Brazil. I had everything already packed so, the morning after the game, I put on a tracksuit and went straight to the airport to catch the flight to Japan where I was to meet the England team before we all flew home to Heathrow.

I was still in my tracksuit expecting to change into my suit in Japan but I didn't get the chance because they had checked my luggage through to the final destination and I couldn't get to my suitcase. Rio Ferdinand and Michael Owen both made a point of mentioning that I was still in a tracksuit when they were expected to travel in suits. The FA officials didn't say anything but I felt a bit underdressed and was a little concerned they would not be impressed. Fortunately, by the time we got to Heathrow, the players had put on casual shirts too.

A few weeks after the end of the tournament the squad was invited to Buckingham Palace to a reception with the Queen. While we were walking through one of the corridors to meet her, I spotted a big chair like a throne at the bottom of the staircase. Kenny Brown, the old West Ham centre half who had been scouting the Japanese side for the tournament while I was scouting in South Korea, had a camera and told me he would take a picture of me sitting on the throne. In return I would take one of him. He had just managed to take my photograph when a security guard came rushing over, loudly remonstrating with us. I still have my photo but poor old Kenny never got his.

We went down into an enormous room to wait for Her Majesty. She was introduced to all the players first and spent a long time chatting to each of them, which I thought was very impressive. She then came over to the coaches and staff and greeted all of us and said to Eriksson, 'I suppose you were as good a player as all of these young lads.'

'No, I wasn't that good, Ma'am,' said Sven.

I leaned down to her as she is quite petite and I towered over her and said, 'He's only being modest, Ma'am.'

Sven went bright red with embarrassment but she gave me a lovely smile as she walked on to greet the rest of the staff.

A LEEDS MISADVENTURE

Although my relationship with England was still very positive and I enjoyed working with them, my direct involvement with the team was declining, when Terry rang me to say that he had been offered the chance to take over at Leeds from David O'Leary, who had just been sacked after a big outcry at Leeds because Rio Ferdinand had been sold to Manchester United. O'Leary had fallen out with Peter Ridsdale, the chairman, and been sacked.

Terry asked if I fancied joining him. As I had nothing else in the pipeline, I agreed but, as Terry's chief scout at the time was Ian Broomfield, I would not take that role. That was not a problem. Terry invited me up for the weekend and booked me into the hotel in which he was staying and together with Ian Broomfield we sat down and discussed my situation with the club and how I would work with Terry and Ian.

I stayed a couple of days to get to know the players and watch the training and it seemed as though Terry had calmed matters down at the club. I felt that he had the players on his side. That was the first time I had worked with Brian Kidd, who was Terry's coach. He had been a legend as a player, both with Manchester United and Manchester City. He was very articulate. After doing a few assessments of our future opponents for Terry, Brian would sit down with me and go through every detail of the opposition. That detailed analysis was Brian's strength.

Terry had a good team on the staff side and players with a lot of potential to take Leeds forward but events beyond his control were to lead to a very different outcome. Given the loss of Rio Ferdinand, it was important that Leeds should retain their best players. While in discussion with Peter Ridsdale, Terry had been promised that Jonathan Woodgate would not be sold but it happened anyway.

I knew then that the writing was on the wall and that Terry was thinking that he had made a mistake in going to Leeds. The results had not gone well and the club was in financial trouble. I attended one of the games and walked into the grounds, where the Leeds supporters were shouting out to me, 'Go back to London, you cockney bastards.' So Yorkshire was not too impressed. It was not long before Terry left the club and I went with him.

Since then, Leeds has continued to struggle to regain the status it had in the Don Revie era and it probably wouldn't have mattered who took over as manager at that time as the outcome would have been the same.

During my time at Leeds I was still involved with England, doing occasional assessments, and then Sven brought in Brian Kidd to join the England coaching staff. Having left Leeds, I carried on assessing individual players for England and assessing opposition teams for the European Cup qualifiers. Brian and I would meet up at training sessions along with Sammy Lee on the coaching staff to discuss our opinions of the players and tactics.

Brian would still take the time to sit down and talk through the opposition with the same attention to detail, so he was an important member of Sven's set-up, although Sven was much less of a hands-on coach than Terry and Bobby Robson had been.

NEW HORIZONS

Time moved on. I was now effectively semi-retired but I hadn't lost any of my enthusiasm for the game. I was regularly asked to attend matches for various teams and stayed in frequent contact with managers and coaches at different clubs, giving my thoughts on players and team performance. Since most of the games were in the evening, I had time to spare during the day when I was not directly involved in a club so I decided to join the local gym and leisure centre at Chalfont St Peter so that I could keep my body active and at the same time help to keep my marbles.

I developed a new interest as I made some good friends in our over-fifties swimming sessions and a small group of five of us go on regular awaydays, travelling on the Eurostar to have lunch in Brussels, Lille or Paris, spending afternoons and evenings at the Windsor Racecourse, enjoying barbecues and pub lunches in the summer, even swimming in the sea in Broadstairs.

It was one of that group, Dawn Franklin, who runs her own business and who, having heard my stories so many times, helped me to put them together and write this book.

Another of the group, Malcolm Head, is a keen racing man and he introduced me to the membership of Windsor Racecourse, where we frequently meet friends from the football world as a lot of football people enjoy horse racing. One afternoon, as Malcolm and I wandered over to the parade ring, Sir Alex Ferguson spotted me, came over and took us into the ring as he had a horse running called Lord of the Shadows.

The trainer, Richard Hannon, thought the horse, a two-year-old, had a great chance and Sir Alex recommended that we put a bet on it. Lord of the Shadows was a lovely horse and went off as odds-on favourite but was beaten by half a length. Sir Alex called me over after the race and said, 'Never mind. You'll get your money back next time.'

I didn't have the heart to tell him that I had backed the winner, Silverheels, having already placed the bet before he recommended Lord of the Shadows.

Little did I know it but my visits to Chalfont Leisure Centre were about to open the chance for me to get back to my roots with non-league clubs and to work again with young players. I was in the gym on the rowing machine when one of the life-guards, a young lad in his twenties, came over and introduced himself as Andy Ackrell, a footballer who had played for the local club, Chalfont St Peter. Apparently he recognised me because I had recently opened the village fete in Harefield, where I now live, and I had donated a signed England shirt for the village raffle. He had bought several tickets hoping, in the event unsuccessfully, to win the shirt.

The lad said he had been talking about me to his club's manager, Danny Edwards, and asked me if I would be willing to come down to do a session with the players. I hadn't been involved with a non-league club since my days at Dulwich Hamlet and Epsom & Ewell so I was interested to see how things had changed.

When I drove into the club a few evenings later, it was like stepping back in time. Danny and the chairman, Denis Mair, welcomed me and before introducing me to the players, asked if I would help them by doing a session now and again. He wanted me to advise Danny how to get the best from his team. When I met the team, they asked me lots of questions about the players I had worked with over the years, particularly Gazza, Shearer, Sheringham, Pearce and Lineker, who were obviously their idols.

They treated me as if I were a celebrity, even though just like them I had started at the bottom. They were all so enthusiastic about my helping them that they convinced me that this was something I would enjoy doing and that I could help them as a team and in some cases as individuals to go further and realise their potential.

So started a relationship with the club that still continues today. After a few training sessions I appreciated what a good coach they had in Danny. His professional playing career had ended with a knee injury so he had taken his UEFA licences and was also working as a sports teacher in West London Academy. He has the potential to be a successful coach at league level.

Working at a club at this level has highlighted for me the level of talent that is available and that lower league clubs should take more time and effort to bring in such young players from non-league and give them a chance to show what they can do. The best way to assess these boys is not to send out their scouts to watch a single game and then find reasons not to take them in. Instead they should take them in for a week, let them train with the pros and see how they do.

I have recommended a number of Chalfont players who have gone on to play for league clubs, such as Charlie Strutton, who went to Wimbledon, Terrell Lewis, who has played for Chesterfield, and Jerome Okimo, who went to Colchester and Stevenage. When Charlie Strutton scored the equalising goal in the FA Cup tie versus York City, I got as big a kick as I did when backing a winning horse in the Derby.

One of the best decisions made by Denis Mair was to bring into the club an under-18 coach, Wayne Hiron, and his under-18 squad, which had been unable to get financing in the Berkshire area. The chairman asked me to take a look at the under-18 squad. I watched a couple of their games and was very impressed with a number of the players, especially as some of them were only fifteen or sixteen years old. I recommended three of the young players to Fulham, one being Jarvis Edobor, but Fulham were not sufficiently impressed to take it any further. I then recommended the same players to Brentford, who were immediately impressed by Jarvis. They played him in five under-21 games and signed him on a pro contract. The other two were invited to come back to Brentford pre-season.

It's great to see young talent coming through from the lower league clubs to keep in touch with the lads as they move up to the professional circuit. I am sure there is the same potential at other non-league clubs.

In 2006, after Sven was sacked, Terry took over as assistant manager for the England team, working for the new manager Steve McClaren, who had been the coach under Eriksson during the 2002 World Cup. There was wild speculation in the press and radio that I would be back on the England scene because of my relationship with Terry and the boys at Chalfont were very excited on my behalf. Although I had a decent relationship with McClaren, he never wanted to sit down and talk players or tactics with me, unlike Brian Kidd and Sammy Lee.

So when he took over the England job and appointed Terry as his number two I felt that he wouldn't want me in the set up. I did mention to Terry when the speculation began that he shouldn't drive himself mad trying to get me back in. It was not a problem for me as I now had plenty of other things to do. So after all the talk of my returning to England for the third time, it never happened.

Although I was perhaps a little disappointed as there is no job quite like working for the England team, I was not particularly unhappy that I was not included at that time. I thought it might be a strain for both McClaren and Terry with Terry having been a successful manager of the England team and now returning as assistant to McClaren.

As it turned out, McClaren's time with England was short and not a success and he and Terry were sacked after failing to qualify for the Euro 2008 championship, with Fabio Capello taking over. I have always felt that if McClaren had been able to benefit more from Terry's experience and worked on his man-management skills instead of being too close to the players, he would have kept his job a bit longer.

LOOKING BACK

Having worked with so many outstanding managers across the years, I inevitably find myself making comparisons and considering their strengths and weaknesses.

Gordon Jago really gave my career a kick-start and I will always be grateful to him for giving me the opportunity to meet so many managers, coaches and players. As a person he was reliable, honest and a gentleman. In my three years at Millwall and Tampa Bay he always listened to me when I recommended players, wherever I found them in the world.

He was a man of his word and if he had agreed a deal, he would always stick to it. Sometimes there were some let-downs along the way when we had agreed terms with a player only for them or their agent to come back demanding more money, in which case Gordon would refuse and would cut the deal dead. He was articulate and good at man management, building the players' confidence when they needed encouragement. But if anyone crossed him or let him down, he would never forget it. We still keep in touch and remain close friends.

I will always appreciate that Keith Peacock offered me the opportunity to get back into the English league by bringing me into Gillingham on my return from Tampa. Keith and I have always had a good relationship and meet up from time to time. He is a loyal friend and a great family man. He supported me on most of my recommendations for players that we brought into Gillingham. He always worked hands-on with the players, even joining in with small-sided games in training and had the ability to bring out the best in a number of young players but sometimes he didn't get the support he deserved within the club.

I didn't have an immediate rapport with David Pleat but after working closely with him I got to appreciate his brilliant tactical awareness and his immense knowledge of the players and the game. He had a tremendous memory, enabling him to recall information about individual players, their skills, their best positions and their potential, even those in the lower league clubs.

Whenever I recommended players, David would want to assess them himself and would form his own opinions. He was technically very good at playing systems, changing systems during the match when the game demanded it. He is highly regarded in the football world and rightly so and, like Gordon and Keith, remains a good friend.

As soon as I worked with Bobby Robson I recognised that he not only knew about the players and the game but he also knew all the backroom staff, right down to the tea ladies. He was also up on the detailed running and financing of the club. He was a good man-manager and knew how to get the best from his players. One odd characteristic was that he would frequently confuse players' names, especially if they were phonetically similar, and this caused some amusement among his listeners. But this was seen as an endearing trait, because he was so well respected as a manager. He always listened to what players had to tell him and appreciated my opinion and, being a Geordie, would take particular interest in players that I had recommended from the north east of England.

Although I worked with Sven-Göran Eriksson for the 2002 World Cup, I didn't really get close to understanding the man. We never developed a warm rapport, which was perhaps because he had not personally brought me into the role. Unlike the other managers I worked with, he always seemed somewhat aloof and never wanted to discuss tactics or the attributes of the opposition.

His focus was always on spending time working and socialising with the players.

For me, Terry Venables was simply the best of the managers I worked with. His soccer brain was always ahead of anyone else's and both Malcolm Allison and Tommy Doherty told me that Terry was demonstrating his football management skills even at an early stage in his career as a young player. He was an amazing man manager, understanding when individual players needed support, encouragement or criticism.

He would sit down with players, like Gazza, when they were going through difficult times with the game or with their families and would give them the guidance they needed. He had an ability to explain even the most complex strategies in simple terms so that the players could understand and focus on the tactics needed.

His half-time talks were legendary; he always had a Plan B and could turn round a game that wasn't going the way he wanted. He never needed to raise his voice; he would keep the players' attention by the clarity of his analysis of the game and his ability to communicate what needed to be done. Terry ensured that all the staff members were closely involved and he and I developed a very close friendship, so much so that I now regard him as almost a member of my family.

PLAYING FOR CHARITY

Terry and I have always kept in regular contact, either by phone or meeting up at the Carlton Tower Hotel in Knightsbridge or Motcombs Brasserie nearby. After Terry and McClaren left England, in the quiet period after the season had finished in 2006, we met at the Carlton Tower when Terry asked me if I would be interested in joining him for a charity programme on ITV called *Soccer Aid* in support of the charity UNICEF.

He said it would be England versus the rest of the world. He would manage England and I would be his assistant manager. I was quite excited at the prospect of working again with Terry and the celebrities who were going to play in the teams, as well as helping the charity. I, like a lot of people in the football world, enjoy getting involved in charity work and get quite a kick out of seeing how we can make a difference to people's lives and generate interest in good causes.

Terry said that Dave Butler would be the physio and David Geddes would be the coach. The celebrities scheduled to take part for England were Robbie Williams, who was the main organiser of the event, the actor Damian Lewis, the presenter Angus Deayton, the musician David Gray, the actor Dean Lennox Kelly, TV and radio presenter Jamie Theakston, World Champion snooker player Ronnie O'Sullivan, TV presenter Ben Shephard, the former footballer and now TV presenter Jamie Redknapp, songwriter Jonathan Wilkes (a good player who could have been a professional footballer) and the entertainer Bradley Walsh. Among the star footballers on the England side were Tony Adams, John Barnes, Les Ferdinand, David Seaman and Gazza.

For the rest of the world, the celebrities were Tony Blair's spin doctor Alastair Campbell (who had a go at me when he saw me reading the *Daily Mail* – obviously, being a Labour supporter, he didn't take to my political views being much more right of centre), rugby player David Campese, French footballer Marcel Desailly, Irish TV presenter Craig Doyle, Dunga, a famous Brazilian midfielder, athlete Ben Johnson, comedian Patrick Kielty, singer-songwriter and ex-member of Westlife Brian McFadden, French international David Ginola, Eddie Irvine the racing driver, Russian ice-hockey player Sergei Fedorov, Lothar Matthäus the former German football captain, chef Gordon Ramsay, Manchester United legend Peter Schmeichel, Gianfranco Zola, who was then managing Watford, and the American actor Alessandro Nivola. Ruud Gullit was to be the manager of the Rest of the World team with Gus Poyet (now manager of Chinese Super League side Shanghai Shenhua) as his assistant. Ant and Dec were to present the programme.

We all met at Bisham Abbey, where I had previously trained with the Rowdies and then with the England squad, and at the Fulham training ground at Motspur Park. I already knew all of the footballers on the England team and I had worked with Bradley Walsh when he had been a player at Brentford and I had been working part-time, helping out Freddie Callaghan on his coaching staff after I came back from America. I was pleasantly surprised that the celebrities seemed very down to earth and excited to be playing football with the football stars.

There was a great atmosphere of camaraderie, with Gazza the life and soul of the party. Right from day one of the two weeks of hard work, Terry showed the same level of commitment as if he were managing Tottenham or the England squad. Terry, the two Davids and I met before training each day. Dave Butler would advise on the fitness of the players and David Geddes and Terry would liaise on how they were to be warmed up and the drills they would go through in that day's training session.

My job was to suss out the celebrities on the Rest of the World side and compare them with the celebrities on our side, identifying their weaknesses and strengths. Because the England team and the Rest of the World teams trained at different times, I would sneak out and, from a vantage point without being too obvious, I would watch the Rest of the World in training.

During the Soccer Aid tournament, both teams and staff were invited to 10 Downing Street for a reception with the prime minister. This was to be my third visit to No. 10. The first had been during John Major's term when he had personally taken Terry, Terry's wife, Evette (who everyone knows as Toots), and me on a private tour around the building, showing us the Downing Street paintings. He seemed to me a perfect gentleman and very knowledgeable about football and cricket.

The second visit had been early in Tony Blair's premiership when the England squad under Sven-Göran Eriksson had been invited to meet the Blairs, Gordon Brown and John Prescott. On that occasion we were lined up on arrival to be greeted by Cherie Blair and her daughter, with Dave Sexton and me standing behind Sven and several FA officials. Cherie greeted Sven and those in front of us, smiled at Dave and me as she was about to shake our hands but, at that moment she spotted David Beckham standing immediately behind me. Cherie and her daughter's faces lit up to see David, and Dave Sexton and I were immediately relegated to the lowest ranks of the celebrity list as we were passed over completely.

On this third visit during Soccer Aid, I did get the chance to have a friendly chat with Tony Blair. I took the opportunity to bring up the subject of rising crime in the country, much of which I put down to poor discipline and a lack of a deterrent. Given my background, I told him that I favoured having a referendum on the reintroduction of capital punishment. He clearly didn't want to pursue the conversation so he replied that it was a much more complex issue than that.

I then changed the subject and mentioned that I had worked with his father-in-law, the actor, Tony Booth, when he was out of work in Smithfield Market, which was clearly also another touchy subject. Terry told me I should be more diplomatic but he knows me well enough to know that if they had given me a list of subjects to avoid, I would probably have raised all of them. I clearly was not going to be invited to Downing Street again during the Blair premiership.

The *Soccer Aid* programme was televised across two weeks, culminating in the final to be held at Old Trafford. My grand-daughters, Jade, Demi and Danielle, were interested when they heard that all the celebrities were coming but they didn't get to meet them and instead had to be satisfied with autographs from Robbie Williams and a few others. In the middle of the programme we heard that Maradona would be flying in to join the Rest of the World team and this news generated some excitement amongst the players, particularly the celebrities who were looking forward to being able to say that they had played against the great man.

The talking point for the final was that Maradona and Gazza would be playing on opposing teams. It was an amazing atmosphere at Old Trafford. The ground was full to capacity with 70 000 spectators and it was actually a good football game that everyone enjoyed and raised millions for the charity.

At half time, I had a chat with Jonathan Wilkes and told him to come off the line and run diagonally against Kielty because Kielty was not a runner and was not strong on his left-hand side. As it turned out our tactics worked a treat because Jonathan did exactly that and scored the winning goal. The England team beat the Rest of the World 2–1 in the final at Old Trafford.

After the game both sides were lining up to receive their medals, which were to be presented by Sir Bobby Charlton, when Terry turned to me and instead of leading the rest of us, he said to me, 'You go up and get your medal first.' The announcer on the tannoy was either having a joke or got confused because he incorrectly introduced me as Sir Ted Buxton, which prompted a few phone calls from friends and from my granddaughters afterwards saying they didn't know I had been knighted.

As Bobby Charlton leaned over to put the medal round my neck, he grabbed my arm and said, 'You've done a great job there.' I felt elated to be part of it.

MATCH (NOT) OVER

Meanwhile at Chalfont, the club has had some success in my time with them, being promoted to the Southern Football League and reaching the semi-finals of the FA Vase.

Reaching the semi-final of the FA Vase was a big thing for the club and the prospect of going on to play in the final at Wembley was a major incentive. We were drawn against Glossop for the match and although a hotel had been arranged, we still had nowhere to train. I left a message for Sir Alex Ferguson and, as he always does, he promptly returned my call. I asked him if he could recommend anywhere and he immediately offered us the use of all the facilities at Carrington, Manchester United's own training ground.

This would have been great for the team but the logistics wouldn't work as we would be travelling up on the Friday and training on the Saturday, when the ground was already committed. Instead, Sir Alex suggested Ashford Town Football Club and put me and Danny in touch with them. They readily offered their facilities. The Chalfont lads were very impressed that someone as busy as Sir Alex would find time to help out a small club, but that's the calibre of the man.

We were all very excited about the prospects of the game and were confident that we could win. The game went well and we were winning 2–1 when we played the extra four minutes of the game. The linesman turned to me and said the time was up but I think the referee was influenced by the home crowd and the home officials and at that moment the referee awarded Glossop a corner instead of blowing to end the game.

The Chalfont fans were shouting to the referee that the time was up and our players started to protest that it wasn't a corner anyway. As a result, our team lost their concentration; the corner was quickly taken and Glossop scored to take the game to penalties. We lost 4–2 on penalties. We were absolutely gutted and I felt as much disappointment at losing to Glossop as I had felt when England lost on penalties to Germany in the 1996 semi-final of the European Cup.

I made my feelings known to the referee and his officials after the game and even the Glossop manager said that they had got out of jail that day and admitted that if he had been in our shoes, he would have felt robbed. It was a long and miserable journey home and the disappointment stayed with me for weeks, as it did for the young players who were crestfallen at losing their chance to play at Wembley.

The start of a new season always brings new hope and aspirations; having been promoted to the Southern League in 2011, the club is on a surer-footing than some other clubs at the same level that are often in a somewhat precarious position. I have high hopes for them and still get a kick out of going to the training ground to work with them and watch their games.

Although I am well past retirement age, I consider myself more than fortunate to be fit and still heavily involved with the game, having done regular assessments at matches for Sunderland and then Fulham, keeping in contact with players I have worked with who are now in management and coaching as well as getting the chance to help youngsters move on in the game.

Football is a very sociable world and I have kept in touch with a lot of players from way back. In 2009 the South London dockers sponsored a Dockers Day when a lot of the old players and staff were invited. It was great to see all the old players together again – fellows like Charlie Hurley, George and Jack Fisher, Pat Brady and all the lads Millwall won promotion with, such as Barry Kitchener, Phil Walker, Terry Brisley and Johnny Seasman.

A few faces of course were missing, notably Ray Goddard, the goalkeeper, who had sadly died some time before. Ray was the one reason Millwall got promotion with all the saves he had made in the last sixteen games during that particular season. Another missing face was Trevor Lee, who at that time no one could locate but who has turned up at subsequent games. After we were all presented on the pitch, the players and staff of the promotion year were presented with replicas of the original championship medals, which rounded off a perfect day.

Looking back now I realise how lucky I have been to have come through the Blitz, to have survived the Malayan campaign and to have spent my career experiencing the most amazing highs and lows in football. The game has gone through enormous change and upheaval in my lifetime, from the days when even top players earned very little but played for the love of the game, when they had to buy their own replacement steel-capped leather boots which had to be broken-in, when the ball was laced-leather and weighed a ton and the games were played on muddy pitches with fans standing on the terraces.

Nowadays, premiership players are all millionaires, sponsors provide new designer kit every season with light-weight high-technology boots and aerodynamic balls, and games are played in stadia with immaculate pitches, floodlights and seated terracing.

I am often asked how the top players of yesteryear compare to the players of today. The likes of Stanley Matthews, Tom Finney and Tommy Lawton had tremendous talent, were passionate about the game and came up the hard way. They all started at the bottom, cleaning boots, painting the terracing and helping out the groundsmen so they knew every aspect of the game and their club. They had great stamina and courage and were made of stern stuff, frequently playing through pain from injuries so that they wouldn't miss a game. Most players had to have another job during the three months of the summer and many of them were taxi drivers, plumbers or worked in pubs.

Top players nowadays are better all-round athletes. They have to devote more time to training and play many more games to keep them at the peak of their ability. Their diets are regulated to maintain the highest fitness levels. Their constant travelling at home and abroad puts them under increased pressure and they have to cope with the stress of public celebrity and constant scrutiny both on and off the pitch so they need high levels of mental strength.

Those old players had the ability to adapt to circumstances so I am confident that, if they had had the advantages of the modern game, they would have been just as successful on the pitch and would give any of the modern day players a run for their money. Whether they would be able to cope with the stresses of modern day celebrity status is a different question.

For myself, I wouldn't have changed a thing. It's been quite a journey for a butcher's boy from Deptford, which has taken me across the world to places and to people I could never have imagined I would encounter. I have had the chance to understand every aspect of the game and to work with the best in the business. Not many people have an opportunity to live a fantastic life like mine. Someone up there must like me.

ACKNOWLEDGEMENTS

I would like to thank Steve Stammers for his help and encouragement to get me started on my book; Dawn Franklin for her tenacity in working with me throughout the writing, sifting through all my recollections and capturing the stories that make up the book and the RedDoor team of Heather Boisseau, Clare Christian and Anna Burtt for their enthusiasm, expertise, flair and hand-holding in bringing the book to publication.

PICTURE CREDITS

Plate 1: p.2 all images © Richard Steinmetz and reproduced with permission

Plate 2: p. 6 photograph of Chalfont St Peter © Ian Doorbar and reproduced with permission; p.7 photograph of Ted with Mark Robson, Gary Lineker and Gary Mabbutt © Ray Pickard and reproduced with permission

INDEX

INDEX

Epsom and Ewell (football club) 42, 44, 47, 127

Eriksson, Sven-Göran 186, 192–193, 197, 203, 206–207

Escape To Victory (movie) 60–61

Euro 96 *see* European Cup, 1996

European Cup
  1979 67
  1996 142, 154–161, 214
    England versus Scotland 154–155
    England versus Holland 155–158

Evacuation during Second World War 7–10

FA Cup Final 1991 (Nottingham Forest v Tottenham) 125–127

FA Vase
  Epsom and Ewell in 44–45, 127, 214
  Chalfont St Peter in 213–214

Fan Zhiyi 172, 177

Farina, Frank 193–94

Farrar, Michelle 164, 193

Fenwick, Terry 113, 114, 188, 190

Ferdinand, Les 209

Ferdinand, Rio 197, 198–99

Ferguson, Alex 118–119, 123, 140, 200–201, 213

Ferguson, Mike 149, 150

Finney, Tom 215

Fisher, George 17, 35, 215

Fisher, Jack (Jackie) 17, 35, 215

Fitzgerald, Ella 82, *pl 1*

Foley, Theo 46, 48, 50, 54, 55, 86–87

Football's Coming Home (song) 155–156

Foreman, Freddie 114

Forsyth, Banger 18

Foss, Dickie 35

Fowler, Robbie 146, 150

Franklin, Dawn 200

Fraser, 'Mad' Frankie 132

Galvin, Tony, 101

Gascoigne, Paul 6, 102, 118–124, 154, 183–184, 211, *pl 1, pl 2*

Geddes, David 208, 209

'George the Baker' 2

Gillingham 83, 85, 92–95, 205, *pl 1*

Goddard, Ray 50, 51, 55, 215

Goldberg, Mark 188–189, 191

Gordon, Jimmy 67, *pl 1*

Gorlow, Mr and Mrs 44

Gorman, John 58, 59, 95, 161, 163, 164

Gough, Richard 101, 107

Graham, George 55, 125, 148, 166

Gray, Phil 111, 112

Gray, Ron 34

Greenwich and District, football trials for 15

Grip, Tord 193, *pl 2*

Gullit, Ruud 209

Hall, Eric 131, 151

Hammam, Sam 186, 187, 188

Hamilton, Bryan 53

Harefield 140, 142, 201

Harford, Mick 187

Harris, Allan 58, 108, 109, 111

Harris, Ronnie (Chopper) 58, 108

Hartley, Trevor 99, 100, 101, 104, 107–108

Haslam, Harry 38–39

Head, Malcolm 200

Healey, Derek 48, 59

Hill, Jimmy 143–144, *pl 2*

Hiron, Wayne 202

Hoddle, Glenn 94, 98, 101, 107, 160, 163–164, *pl 1*

Hodge, Steve 101

Holland vs England game 1996 155–158

Honduras, visit to 71–73

Hong Kong Eleven (football team), England friendly with 144

Houghton, Bobby 40

Howard, Ron 99, 103

Howe, Don 135, 150, 156, 170–171

Hubert, Walter 133, 134

Iran games (as technical director China team) 176, 177–178

Israel, trip to 133–135

INDEX

ABOUT THE AUTHOR

Edward 'Ted' Buxton is a football scout and coach with over
forty years' experience. He spent three years with the Tampa Bay
Rowdies, who twice won their division in the North American
Soccer League. As technical director of China's national football
team he took them to the Asian Cup quarter-final and World Cup
qualifiers.

Ted has worked regularly with football royalty, including Terry
Venables and Sven-Göran Eriksson for the England squad. He
has been involved with *Soccer Aid* and instead of slowing down
at retirement age, continues to scout for various league clubs
and to advise non-league clubs including Chalfont St Peter. His
previous book *Soccer Skills for Young Players* has been published in
various countries.